RAMPS
or How to Take a Leek in the Woods
by Brian Cool

Contact: email - becool@netpenny.net

Blog – www.becool2112.wordpress.com

ISBN-10: 1484072162

ISBN-13: 978-1484072165

for Joe

THE WILD WOOD LEEK.
Strongest of Spring's ephemerals
Just one-a-day raw, they say
To keep the doctor and the nurse
Keep the teacher too
And everyone else away

Contents

PREFACE—ABOUT THIS BOOK

Let's call this the first edition of what I hope will remain the most complete guide to the pursuit of the wild ramp. It is a distillation of ten seasons of harvesting them for income, and a lifetime of enjoying their flavor. This book is dedicated to a man whose wisdom and influence is felt on its every page, friend and fellow wildcrafter Joe Snow.

Here you will find a full description of the plant and its lifecycle. Here are in-depth descriptions of harvesting procedures, cleaning, uses and preservation. Leek lore and history are contrasted with study and fact. I also cover the basics of business for those commercial harvesters out there, and how it is possible with a conscience clear of sustainability issues. And of course, tips on cooking and a handful of essential recipes.

The book's title comes from an old word for wild garlic or onion, "ramson". Used by early immigrants to the southern Appalachian Mountains, it was first mentioned in English print around the middle of the sixteenth century. Rendered by the nuances of dialect, rams or ramson, has become today's ramp. Many antecedents of the word exist because of its wild European cousins.

A writer likes it when a thing can be called by more names than one (don't ask why), while taxonomists hate such blasphemy. Throughout this book, I will call them variously ramps, leeks or Allium tricoccum. It is hard to nail down one name for such a widespread plant. French-Canadian names are ail debois or ail sauvage. Native Americans have called them shikaakwa and Bagawaj zhigaagawinzhiig . . . which in itself may explain why the names haven't grown to prominent usage.

In describing the taste, you will find comparisons to various onion relations, shallots, scallions etc. They look like a cross between onions, leeks and garlic—they are none of the above.

I've eaten them since early childhood, just like a lot of other folks whose families have roots here in northwest Michigan. Much depends on where you live; say "wild onion" and some people think you mean Allium cernuum, the nodding onion, others think you're talking about the subject of our book here. We always just called them leeks. I guess we live deep enough 'in the sticks' that we don't say *wild* leeks.

Knowledge about the uses of ramps, and their place in the woods has long been hard to distill from the mass of misinformation available. The purpose of this book is to spread understanding of a powerful plant—its lifecycle, health benefits, basic techniques and options for its use as food, planting and sustainable harvest methods, and income potential for wildcrafters.

Ramps

It is also worth emphasizing now, that I have imagined a bold future for the humble and wild leek—a future where we do not force it down the old worn road to endangerment—a future that relies on the tools of moderation and modern communication. This guidebook was developed with the hope that with care and sense, we can promote the use of one of nature's tastiest gifts without driving it onto the growing list of at-risk species.

Many landowners, in addition to using their property as a place to live or work, enjoy the cultural and natural resource values of their parcel. If you have a place with hardwoods, ramps can provide an opportunity to connect with a rich history in a direct way. If you don't already have them in your woods you can start some. Voluntary stewardship is of great importance to existing and future uses, but such efforts are many times more effective when fueled by information.

Whether seven generations from now or seventy, our grandchildren deserve the chance to forage for these and other wild edible foods that make up a major part of our distant past. In planning this book, I had a goal to inspire people to get into the woods more often. It's good for your spirit, good for your health, and if you can rustle up some grub (not necessarily grubs mind you) while you're out there, so much the better.

Note: The following abbreviations are used throughout; FiTW—Found in The Woods (a small business owned by my wife), NTFP—Non-Timber Forest Product, NMG—Niche Market Good.

INTRODUCTION, "MEET AL TRICOCCUM"

An introduction to Ramps should begin with their smell, or *odeur* as detractors might say with noses pinched. More easily found by smell than by sight, they produce a powerful and distinctive aroma—onion doubled, tinged with crushed garlic and earth.

Old-timers from around these parts (the eastern half of rural North America or thereabouts) can relate the same story from their one-room schoolhouse days of some 'innocent' kid, "eating the little stinkers on the walk to school," and being summarily sent home for the day! Even the back of the class wouldn't do.

"It's the breath!" Funny stuff that . . .

Of all the places that they grow, the Appalachian tradition is richest in lore, and smelly humor. One devoted website lovingly dubs them, the 'King of Stink'.

So why then would anyone want to eat them? Well, if you cook them right they are delicious! That's the main reason. We will get to the others. However, if you dare eat one raw, I'm sure you have your reasons.

Ramps dwell in that dark mysterious corner behind our brains where the hunter-gatherer in us lurks, disdained by some, overlooked by many, a joy to thousands, a moneymaker for others.

They dwell in the deep woods where I have witnessed an unbroken field of their lush green stretching away in all directions as far as I could see. Early in spring, they come forth, chancing bitter winds and late snows to catch what sun they can before the trees leaf-out, and by early summer, every trace of them has all but disappeared, the sunshine stored away underground.

And they dwell in danger of over-harvest, something for which our species has shown an awful capacity, and with less technology and far fewer people working at it than now.

Ramps (*Allium tricoccum* or *Allium tricoccum* var. *burdickii*), are native to much of eastern North America. Their range extends across Canada's southern provinces of Manitoba, Ontario, New Brunswick, Quebec and Nova Scotia, to northern New England from Maine south to Delaware, south to North Carolina and Maryland, in the uplands of Georgia and Tennessee, west and north to Missouri and Illinois, and everywhere in between.

They are found growing in patches or clumps in rich, moist, deciduous forests. In earliest spring, smooth, broad green leaves rise from an onion-like bulb. The leaves wither and disintegrate before the flowers appear in May, June or July. Atop a naked stem, small creamy-white flowers form a small domed cluster, which becomes a crown of black pearls as seeds mature.

Fresh ramps aren't up for long, but you can easily collect enough to preserve some for later. Or you can make note of where to find them later in the year. Spring leek bulbs, though smaller, do have a certain tenderness that later bulbs don't. Larger older bulbs are possibly even tastier, though they do benefit from some extra cooking time.

The bulbs have the taste of a sassy onion, which may not be to everyone's liking, but to those who shun them, "Hey . . . more for us." The leaves also have an onion taste, though milder. For certain people, the raw leaves are said to cause gastric upset—nobody I know though.

Maybe there was no way they could have known that their actions would leave us with a wounded world. Our ancestors wouldn't have known what to do with the gimcrack of modern life. Their diet was fished, farmed, gathered on the run, killed fresh or scavenged. No GMOs, no synthetics, no growth hormone injections, no antibiotics, herbicides, food coloring, corn syrup derivatives, pink slime, chemical preservatives or irradiation. In other words, none of the crutches of science.

Must we take the whole world in our clutching grasp, believing that we can do no wrong, or that it doesn't matter? I shudder to think of a time ahead when the above list is but the beginning in our move away from nature's ways, mostly to make up for the very loss of biodiversity for which we alone are responsible.

In an era when most of us live close to a grocery store, hunting has become an *add*-venture through the butcher's display case, and foraging in the produce aisle has become the modern norm. However, the woods are still full of free food, and some few are still determined to make dinner of it. Wild onions (not necessarily A. tricoccum) have traditionally been one of the most widely important food sources that man has known, probably because they are nutritious and packed with flavor.

Nowadays, they bring the high dollar from chefs *in the know*, and at farmers' markets in the city. They have entered the strange land of the non-timber forest product niche market good. And foraging, like pastured poultry, farmers' markets and community supported agriculture, has been reawakened as a 'locavore' fixation.

Granted they are not an obvious candidate for such attention at first glance. Lowly and trampled upon they are, small and smelly, early as Spring's first birds, born in out of the way places. The bulb looks like a baby onion, the leaf a green banner.

Must be something in that over-strong flavor.

Add ramps (sparingly) to rice dishes, potato dishes, bean dishes and in almost any recipe calling for regular garden leeks, garlic or onions. A taste that only the forest can impart has created a singular delicacy. And cause for celebration, no less; events devoted to their ironic allure attest to the importance of this plant.

Clumps form patches.

LORE & USAGE

Ramps Galore

In the land of mined mountaintops
In the land of hardscrabble farm
Of perched roads and hiker's yarn

In the land of green mountain ski resort
Of blue ridges and primeval forest
And peripheral beauty

The hill folk have something won
The ramp in all its lowly glory
Makes a meal tell a story

Of the fight for naming rights and more
Go and search for 'wild leeks'
And you'll find ramps, galore

"Onions, leeks and garlic have been regarded as curatives for an infinite variety of ailments as far back as the Egyptians. The Chinese, Greeks and Romans used them for relieving worms, indigestion, symptoms of old age, skin diseases and respiratory ailments. To most Europeans garlic and onions are the proverbial cure-all, even today." National Onion Association

"Man esteems himself happy when that which is his food is also his medicine." Alma R. Hutchens

Wild leeks with fresh trout. A meal to remember!

Ramps are great to eat just like onions or garlic. They are usually prepared quite simply fried in butter or fat with scrambled eggs and/or sliced potatoes. They are used in soup, sandwiches, salad, casseroles, pasta, pizza, chili and go good with almost any meat. They can also be preserved for later use. It's easy to gather and freeze a supply of these plants for use throughout the year—drying and storing is easy too. Another good preservation technique is pickling in vinegar.

There are so many ways to use ramps that a person could only hope to try them all. My own experience with them includes a long list of ways to eat them, which we'll cover in a later chapter, but like many other plants they are useful to man as medicine too. Whispers of anti-cancer properties in selenium-enriched ramps have the medical community interested in a plant that has been used curatively by those close to the land for years.

In temperate climates around the world, the first plants to emerge in the spring take on a traditional role in man's diet. Such plants provide necessary vitamins and minerals after long winter months without fresh vegetables. They don't come much earlier than ramps.

Folk traditions in the southern Appalachians came to guide the gathering and use of ramps, and grew into annual spring festivals. Such occasions draw locals and tourists alike to enjoy the rich history of a little plant.

I believe that the many annual spring ramp festivals exist because of a deep respect for and understanding of man's place in the world, and in his community. The tremendous volume of ramps consumed at these festivals is gathered from the forests yes, but that only strengthens my belief that we won't eat them out of existence. Such occasions, by their very existence, might inspire a much-needed conservation effort.

In rural settings where ramps grow and where incomes are often low, such an accompaniment to inexpensive dishes can understandably cause excitement. But ramps are not limited to fare for us of the lower 96%—professional foragers can make a name among chefs who demand wild foods. The demand caters to an eclectic taste for rare and expensive flavor experiences. Comparable to leeks on that list are the fiddlehead fern, the morel mushroom and many more.

Upscale restaurants around the world use this plant as an exotic ingredient in an elegant meal. So, hundreds of gatherers harvest millions of them, and aside from one confirmed ramp farm, it's all wild. In Tennessee, Québec, and a growing list of other places this plant has become so over-harvested that conservation measures have been necessary. In other places, the harvesters themselves have voluntarily adopted sustainability principles.

The author in his element.

Foraging is trendy with the growing locavore food movement, but we may look to the past to find many more uses than food for the forest's bounty. Many of us are too remote from the real processes of food production, let alone foraging. We owe it to ourselves and to whatever it is that we consume, to educate ourselves about everything we take into our bodies. Some would say that we even owe it to everyone involved in the chain of distribution that ultimately ends at our plates.

OUR DEEPEST ROOTS

Ramps were important to native people's diets long before the first white settlers. Tribal members gathered the bulbs and leaves of ramps with due respect. Tribal elders taught that gathering should be in amounts of only what is needed so that enough plants remain to ensure their long-term survival. Such advice is timeless.

The wood leek has long been important in the Great Lakes region. When Father (Pere) Jacques Marquette journeyed with his followers from Wisconsin to near the present Chicago, their chief nourishment was wild onion. In fact, the name Chicago is derived from the Indian word "She-khe-ony" for a locality where wild leeks are abundant. *So say some*—another story puts it differently. Others say the city of Chicago took its name directly from the plant itself, called shikaakwa in the language of area's native tribes. Others say the city's name originated from the Indian word for skunk.

Michigan has a Chicago Lake and a Chicagon Lake, neither of which were named after the windy city, but the names of all three could be etymologically related. Our northern Michigan Indian brothers call them, "Bagawaj zhigaagawinzhiig."

As a child, I loved to take to the woods and fields and wetlands on long hikes, snacking on the wild fruits I found there and enjoying nature. I still do that. I've learned to identify more plants though (as well as places that may have been sprayed, like power lines and railways etc). It was on one of these hikes, which were often led by my father until I gained confidence to go on my own, that I learned about the leek. We were looking for morels—finding only a few. Dad seemed quite proud to introduce me to the trailside delicacies, which we promptly took home to cook with our mushrooms. Been hooked ever since.

Kids love to forage.

If you are lucky enough to be taught early by someone knowledgeable about wild foods, great. If not, get a copy of Euell Gibbon's "Stalking the Wild Asparagus," and go from there. Learn about your local plants; habitat, season, look-alikes etc. Take a class, join a club or subscribe to one of the many You-tube wildcrafter channels.

Foraging can be an extension of gardening, or even a part of it. The purslane, sheep sorrel, lamb's-quarters and pigweed we pull up and compost are as good as the crops we take the trouble to cultivate! Dandelions have six times more vitamin A than lettuce, and are also high in calcium, iron, potassium and vitamin C. But even when it can be as easy as weeding the garden most people simply don't think about them, they dismiss foraging as not worth the effort.

All of the cultivated fruits and vegetables we eat today were once *wild* foods. Before gardening there was gathering. Foraging for wild foods can still be an important part of living off the land. As part of a self-sufficient philosophy; it can be a valuable skill, and an intellectual exercise. People do it to save money, and as an enjoyable leisure-time family activity.

If a food culture can be ascribed to something as general as homesteading, eating with the seasons is one of the rules—which means to eat what's growing in the garden, or what's being produced by the live-stock, or what has been preserved or stored in the root cellar. And it usually involves gathering the fat of the land; wild herbs and edibles, wild game and fish.

Be a forager (doesn't mean be a trespasser). Ask permission for access to property. Forage for weeds, fungi, and succulents in your gardens and yards. Go easy on public lands. Practice and encourage conservation and cultivation of wild native foods. When you make them part of your life you will find the value in protecting the plants you use.

Avoid unpleasant surprises by sticking with the easy ones at first. The chance of being sickened or even killed is why we must learn to identify plants.

If you plan to get into the business of selling wild foods, you join a long-heralded group of self-respecting individualists. We are an opportunistic and resourceful bunch. And we are as filled with regret as anyone else when our collective actions cause environmental harm. Who among today's wildcrafters wouldn't wish that ginseng had been managed sustainably all these years. Ginseng and a dozen others; trillium, lady's slipper, goldenseal, blue cohosh

23

(black too), blood root, Echinacea, peyote, slippery elm, sundew, unicorn both true and false, wild ginger and more.

This continent's native people lived a life of interdependence in the forests for many generations. Study confirms stories of their physical endurance. Only 25% of their diet was cultivated. They used plants as food, clothing, instruments, decoration and more. Archaeology finds scant evidence of our latter-day bone deficiencies, cavities, arthritis, tuberculosis, etc.

Remember the man who watched as a long line of people milled outside a city soup kitchen. Later, he found half a dozen species of edible plants there that had been trampled into the ground.

Me and my wild friends.

ALLIUM MEDICINE

Many edible plants possess strong antibacterial properties, in some cases being equal to or even surpassing the power of prescribed antibiotics. These natural medicines have been used for ages, compared to our modern medicines, which are not complex enough to ensure that bacteria do not in time become resistant to them.

Antibiotics have a much simpler chemistry than plant medicines. Yarrow, for instance contains more than 120 different compounds all of which exist in powerful evolutionary balance with each other. All of which work to potentiate, enhance, and mitigate each other's medicinal effects. All alliums (garlic, onions, scallions, shallots, and, to a lesser degree, chives) are rich in sulfur compounds and have antibacterial qualities. Garlic, (Allium sativum) contains over 30 sulfur compounds and 17 amino acids.

Pharmaceuticals, in contrast, are usually quite simple substances, and because of this, bacteria can evolve to counteract their effects. If any one plant straddles the boundary between food and medicine, it is garlic. Dubbed 'nature's penicillin', garlic has been used for as long as humans have recorded history. It has evolved over centuries of cultivation. Horticulturists call it a 'cultigen' because it is not found in the wild.

The onion has been called a more potent germ destroyer than garlic, horseradish, mustard, or hot peppers. Historically, the concentric layers of the onion were believed to draw contagious diseases from the patient into the bulb. Thus, an onion was often hung in a sickroom.

Some of the things we eat seem more medicine than food. Regular use of garlic and onions as herbal antibiotics, in the daily diet help to maintain the overall health of the body. They remain active against the major antibiotic-resistant bacteria. And unlike many other herbs, garlic is directly effective against both bacterial and viral infectious agents—remember that, next time you get the flu. Garlic works well for stimulating immune function and for lowering cholesterol counts and blood pressure either raw, cooked or encapsulated. Raw garlic or its juice kills bacterial infections on contact.

Ramps have been used as folk medicine (my favorite kind) for the same things and in many of the same ways as onions and garlic.

Deadline draws near and I still haven't got my hands on a list of A. tricoccum's active constituents. I guess that's what second editions are for. I can only assume that they share many of the same compounds as garlic and onions, lots of sulfides and such. I assume so not just because the wild leek appears to be the perfect cross between the two, in appearance as well as in taste and smell (though not in life span), but also because of the stories. Lore has it they are a cure for colds and more.

ALLIUM USES THRU THE AGES

Folk Medicine uses the onion as Stimulant, Antiseptic, Diuretic, Tonic and Carminative.

Native Americans reportedly ate raw onions to induce sleep.

To restore the natural color of brown hair, make a rinse of leeks. Boil a few leeks in water for 20 minutes, then strain out the solids. Use the water as a final hair rinse.

Crushed wild leek bulbs applied to the skin as a poultice were used by Native Americans to relieve the pain from bee and wasp stings.

Native Americans used a tea from the bulbs as a wash for open sores. For infected cuts, wounds and abrasions, mash and squeeze to express the juice. Apply juice after washing infected area with soap and water. They also applied bruised wild leek bulbs and stems as a poultice to carbuncles.

Externally: The juice of a grated or bruised onion or leek, with the addition of a little salt, when laid on fresh burns or scalds draws out the fire and prevents them from blistering. Used with vinegar it diminishes skin blemishes.

Experiments show that chewing a raw onion for five minutes renders the lining of the mouth completely free of all harmful bacteria. This practice may not however improve one's breath. Today many mouthwashes and throat lozenges include a synthetic equivalent of the active bacteria-killing property in onion juice.

The use of onions as an antiseptic for ear infections is ancient and universal. Bake an onion until soft—when it has cooled to body temperature, apply to your aching ear, cover with cloth or bandage, and attach with tape.

Russians boil an onion for five minutes, squeeze it, and put both juice and pulp in the ear. Warm mashed garlic, papaya, and pumpkin have also been used thus in various folk medicines.

Feed a cold, and fight it too; make a sandwich of whole wheat bread, grated raw leeks, a thick layer of horseradish and cheese. Also, try chicken broth steaming hot and seasoned with leeks (added after the brew has been taken off the fire).

Legendry of the Middle Ages says necklaces of onions were frequently worn by women to insure good health.

An old Russian custom was to wear a piece of garlic or onion around the neck, chest high, on a string. Which they insisted, kept colds, infections, etc. at bay. Scientific, merit is found for this strange idea in a chemical antiseptic that many plants produce as volatile oils for atmospheric protection.

Eat a whole raw leek to fight a respiratory infection, then chew parsley for the breath. Take fennel or ginger tea if they upset your stomach.

As a domestic medicine the onion, in various preparations, has come to the rescue in colds and croups. Roast an onion until soft, extract the liquid, add honey to taste, mix well and give in teaspoonful amounts as age and condition calls for. Or the whole roasted onion can be eaten with honey.

Onions are helpful in breaking up mucus in the throat, lungs and nasal passages. Better yet, use garlic, onions, and leeks along with herbs regularly to prevent colds and infections.

The Chippewa combined the bulb of Allium tricoccum with blue cohosh (Caulophyllum thalictroides) root, made a tea and used it as an emetic.

Onions can improve kidney function.

If taken raw on an empty stomach, onion and garlic will often clear the digestive system of unwanted creatures.

Tests on humans have demonstrated that onions somehow raise the blood's capacity to dissolve deadly internal clots. Horses suffering from blood clots in their legs have been treated with garlic and onions.

Ancient Egyptians were said to have taken their marriage oath with their right hand on an onion, indicating it was a symbol of eternity because of its formation of a sphere within a sphere.

Patches on patches

WILD FOOD VALUES

Wild foods improve meals at home and while camping, or exploring. Just remember to identify everything before you pick it and you will never have trouble.

In his book Skills for Taming The Wild, Bradford Angier lays bare the life of the traditional outdoorsman. If you were ever lost in the wilderness with just his book and the clothes on your back, you might stand a chance of living, instead of just surviving. And as he explains, countless modern men have not survived the unforgiving world that was once a garden to us. When frontiersmen, prospectors, and others began daring the western plains and deserts of North America, many of them starved in the midst of plenty because they didn't know what to eat or how to prepare it.

Angier advises those fishermen and hikers who want to get a few miles deeper into remote country, "with careful planning you can save weight and space on nearly every item in your pack. When it comes to grub, however, you're still going to need a minimum of 2¼ pounds of reasonably water free provisions daily."

He advises foraging for up to half of what you expect to eat out there. He also tells why we should eat wild when at home. "If you have ever sat down to a well prepared meal that included wild vegetables, maybe you've noticed that many of them seem to taste better than domesticated varieties. You may as well know the trade secret. They *are* better." The food values of some greens diminish as much as one third during the first hour after picking. Granted, most lettuces are packed in the field and shipped the same day, but they still can't compete with what you can gather fresh from nature's garden, or from your own.

<u>NUTRITION VALUE:</u> Robert Shosteck author of How Good *Are* Wild Foods? (Mother Earth News) offered the following information about the nutritional value of foraged edibles.

"Although most foragers have assumed right along that the gratuitous fare—free of additives and genetically untampered with—is naturally wholesome, the increased public interest in wild food plants has created a demand for some hard facts on the nutritional quality of such edibles."

He continues, "A typical male adult, for example, needs 5,000 I.U. (International Units) of vitamin-A per day, and he can get much more than that in a scant half-cup of cooked dandelion greens! Or take that bane-of-the-farmer, amaranth: Just 10 ounces of the leaves or tips of this prolific plant can provide an adult's daily calcium needs, plus almost *all* the iron requirement for men and half that for women."

Shosteck provided a list of eighty popular wild foods and their respective nutrition counts. Values for A. tricoccum are listed below, per 100 gram serving (about five medium ramps):

Calories-52 // Protein-2.2g // Fat-0.3g //Calcium-52mg // Phosphorus-50mg // Iron 1.1mg // Sodium-5mg // Potasium-347mg // Vitamin A-40 I.U. // Thiamine-0.11mg // Riboflavin-0.06mg // Niacin-0.5mg // Vitamin C-17mg

ECOLOGY

When used as a verb applied to plants, the word ramp means to grow and spread luxuriantly. One of North America's finest spring ephemerals—they are elusive denizens of the deciduous forests, where the deep damp rich soil nourishes them. Spears of purple and green emerge from perennial bulbs in late March or early April, before the tree canopy develops. Groups of leaves spread out in mats across the land, hiding the ground completely. By late May the multitude of leaves die back as an occasional flower stalk emerges. Incredibly, their entire annual photosynthetic phase is accomplished in about eight weeks.

Patches as far as the eye can see, *with all them trees in the way.*

SHEETS OF GREEN

When conditions are right for growth, and remain so for long stretches of time, large patches may be so abundant that there seems to be no end to them. Laced throughout the patch will be other plants, and flowers of yellow, white, pink and violet. Ramps prefer a mixed hardwood habitat, thriving in association with other water-loving understory plants including goldenseal, Jack in the pulpit, blue cohosh, Dutchmen's britches, May apple, trillium etc.

In fraternity: trout lily, bloodroot, Solomon's seal, wild violet and ramps.

The leaves are deep green, five to ten inches long, tapering at either end. A long tapering spine divides the leaf lengthwise. The lower end becomes a thin reddish purple stalk (petiole). Underground in the 'rhizosphere' is found a small white elongated bulb up to 2½ inches in length and ¾ inch in diameter.

In June, flowers bloom atop a stiff leafless seed-stalk. it seems designed to lift the ripening seeds just high enough so that they eventually topple over to germinate away from the mother plant. Ants also disperse seeds.

Three seed stalks in midsummer. Kinda hard to see I know.

A PALE TWIN

A. tricoccum var burdickii is similar with slightly smaller flowers (and smaller seed production) and a white or light-green petiole, although color is not a sure identifier of the species. They are reputed to be somewhat milder. I have never seen them outside a patch of their more common cousin. I have also never seen them make up a significant percent of the overall ramp population. Further, I have never seen groupings of clumps. They are so few and far between that I almost never harvest them.

Burdickiis, or 'blondies' on right.

EDIBILITY

The entire plant smells like garlic and onion. Wild leeks possess a unique taste, a cross between a strong scallion, garlic and leek, with nuances not found elsewhere, hence their culinary appeal. Both the bulb and leaf are eaten although the leaf has a somewhat milder flavor. There are rare reports of upset stomach from eating the leaf.

Personally, I have eaten the leaves many times with no ill effects. The leaves tend to toughen later in the season and the tips may yellow. Bulbs are edible year around, but they also get tougher to chew as it gets later it the year.

By the way, their stems aren't really stems. They disappear every year along with the leaves because they are actually part of the leaf (called a petiole). The petiole is also edible and tasty, and often eaten with the rest of the plant.

Rare old four leafed plants. The petioles are quite thick because they are layered like the bulbs—each leaf adds another layer.

UNDERGROUND

Ramps survive by sleeping together. That is, sticking together and sleeping most of the year away underground. When you do see them, you will almost never see a single plant growing outside of a clump and you will almost never see a clump growing outside of a larger patch (though that may not be true at the outer edges of their range).

Dig up a clump and wash off the dirt without breaking the bulbs apart and you will see that many of them are common to a number of branching rhizomes and that the roots of all are an entangled mess.

Clumps destined for transplanting.

When harvesting, we look for larger leaves because they often have a bigger bulb below. They add up quicker. Also, larger bulbs have probably already had the chance to produce seeds. We will often find the remains of the previous year's seed-stalks attached to the base of big bulbs.

Ramps live under constant barrage from above. Dead branches and leaves from the canopy overhead bury everything on the forest floor. The so-called ephemerals have the task of pushing up through whatever may have fallen on them. Some push up with a blunt but forceful instrument, others snake up through with clever tendrils. Ramps form a sharp spear, which is thrust up slowly but surely—through bark, leaves and even rotting wood.

Bulbs rest in a cocoon like sack. It is actually just the oldest outside layer, like an onionskin. This skin has evolved as a cast off with a purpose. It retains moisture, protects the bulb, and as it rots, it feeds the plant.

We often find earthworms intertwined among the roots. In fact, we've seen the baby earthworms inside the skin that encloses the bulb, well protected there by the strong juices, and well fed. It is symbiosis in action as each clump of leeks is home to a family of worms and each family of worms is provider to the plants. Ramps love calcium. Calcium allows plants to take up nitrogen, which in turn promotes leaf growth and assists with protein synthesis and other vital functions. Earthworms not only transform available calcium to a form more easily absorbed by plants, they produce calcium in their calciferous glands during digestion, adding it to the soil as castings.

Bulbs with skins on.

A little known species called Ramsonia Giganticus, found only in the secret Valley of the Ramps.

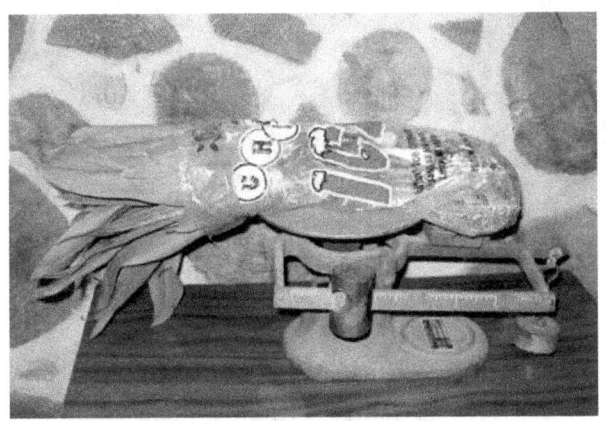

16 ramps from one clump—almost a pound.

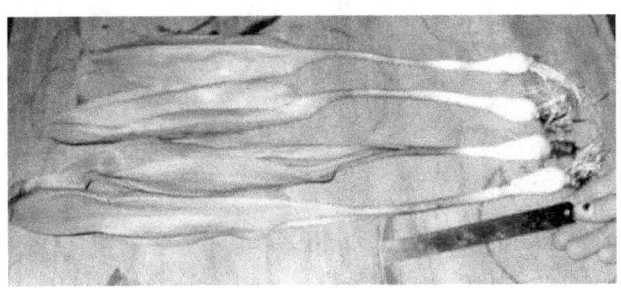

The heaviest one we've found—39 grams, 99centimeters tall.

INFO: ALLIUM TRICOCCUM
Distributional Range

Native: North America

Central to Eastern Canada: - New Brunswick, Nova Scotia, Quebec [s.e.],Ontario, [s.] Manitoba

Northeastern USA: - Connecticut, Indiana, Maine, Massachusetts, Michigan, New Hampshire, New Jersey, New York, Ohio, Pennsylvania, Rhode Island, Vermont, West Virginia

North-Central USA: - Illinois, Iowa, Minnesota, Missouri, North Dakota [e.], South Dakota [e.], Wisconsin

Southeastern USA: - Alabama [n.], Delaware, Georgia [n.], Kentucky, Maryland [w.], North Carolina [w.] Oklahoma, South Carolina [n.w.], Tennessee, Virginia and the District of Columbia

Common Names

English

wild leek, spring onion
ramson, wood leek
wild onion, wild garlic
ramp

French (Canadian)

ail des bois
ail sauvage

Classification

Kingdom Plantae – Plants
Subkingdom Tracheobionta – Vascular plants
Superdivision Spermatophyta – Seed plants
Division Magnoliophyta – Flowering plants
Class Liliopsida – Monocotyledons
Subclass Liliidae
Order Liliales
Family Liliaceae – Lily family
Genus Allium L. – onion
Species Allium tricoccum Aiton – ramp
And A. tricoccum var Burdickii

Threatened & Endangered

In Canada, ramps are a threatened species in Quebec. A person may have ramps in his or her possession or may harvest for personal consumption a quantity not exceeding 200 grams of any of its parts OR a maximum of 50 bulbs or 50 plants annually. The protected status also prohibits buying or selling ramps. Failure to comply with these laws is punishable by a fine.

This plant is listed as a Species of Special Concern in Maine and Rhode Island (and Tennessee where it is also listed as Commercially Exploited). On a side note, Arkansas lists them as a Noxious Weed.

Seeds still on stalk from previous year.

Details

Stem: stemless except for the flower stalk which is smooth, dark green, up to 3 dm tall.

Leaves: Basal, 20 to 30 cm, lance-elliptic, shiny, thick, parallel veined. Green, with deep purple or burgundy tints on the petiole. When bruised they smell like onions. Young plants have only one leaf, older plants have two or three, the oldest have four.

Flower Type: white, three petals, three sepals, born on thick pedicels in a terminal umbel, early summer. They appear after leaves have died.

Fruit/Seed: small spherical shiny black capsules. Summer.

Roots: yellowish brown rhizome with many fibrous rootlets.

Bulb: white, with outer skin.

General: common perennial herb, grows in clumps.

Habitat: grows in rich maple beech forests.

Season of Availability: whole plant collected in spring. Bulbs collected in summer.

Lookalikes: The foliage of the lily of the valley somewhat resembles ramps. Any similar poisonous plants do not smell of onion.

Toxicity: none recorded.

KNOW RETURN

Few data are available on the seasonal and climatic factors that influence ramps. A comprehensive record of the beginning dates of emergence, and of flowering, and of the major atmospheric and weather variations associated with these dates is easily compiled and becomes uniquely useful.

Another kind of study could investigate the economic activity based on sales of ramps.

If harvesters would keep track of a few related factors on a one page 'Seasonal Evaluation Sheet', it would certainly help them. If the information from a number of harvesters were entered into a nationwide database, it would prove invaluable.

Thankfully, the idea for such a study exists in the Ramp Project. At the Ramp Project website, you will find a number of interesting and useful resources, links to literature, history, a bibliography and more.

"We are trying to identify the people who are involved in the collection, distribution and marketing of these products. We are conducting interviews and surveys of folks involved with the collection, trade and use of ramps to better understand their perceptions and attitudes toward managing forests for these edible products. Cultural views and attitudes shape the way people treat natural resources. We hope to learn how forests can be better managed to ensure that the collection of ramps continues to be an integral part of rural lives."

"This [Ramp Project] is also working to determine the quantity of ramps that are eaten and sold each year. By knowing the amount of ramps that are consumed each year, forest managers can better determine if collection is exceeding the rate at which new plants are growing."

Rate of growth, age of sexual maturation, average and maximum longevity, average duration and rates of germination and of seed dispersal; all of these and others are valid topics for more study. These kinds of data can be collected from observations in nature, but much the same questions can be asked about farmed ramps. The answers obtained in one situation may not always be valid in the other, but still worthwhile for comparison.

Occasional studies have been done on ramps. Articles and papers about them are easy to locate. There was once a documentary on public TV out east. But really, little is known about them by the average man on the street. Even among commercial harvesters, there can be a general lack or even suppression of knowledge. If I am allowed to draw any conclusions from the demise of other similar wild food sources, I think that there may be trouble ahead.

Plant science and professional assessments have the best chance of making an impact on conservation efforts, if such assessments determine that such efforts are needed. The sooner studies are done, and regulations put in place, the better the chance that those who depend on ramps in one way or another can continue to do so. I suspect regulations will be called for in one state after another—more as a late response to obvious overharvesting however, than as an action to preserve wildcrafting jobs.

HOW & WHEN TO HARVEST

". . . people disturb the surrounding ground less than a turkey or deer. In my opinion, most people and groups are smart enough to leave enough plants to reseed an area."From the King of Stink website

First, never let it be said that I didn't advise you to dress for the weather, and take extra dry clothes.

Geared up for a day in the woods. Counter clockwise from left Karen, Kim, Joe and Brian, before we got matching outfits☺.

Whether for profit or for personal use, there are a couple of basic methods of harvest to know. There's a pickin' and there's a diggin'. You will decide which method to use based on circumstance and preference. A third method consists of harvesting the leaves alone.

Left on one's own with a forked stick, and some elbow grease, anyone can get a pocketful of leeks out of the ground and back to camp to fry up with those morels. Beyond that it is good to have some technique and a little practice. You can buy a special tool, though I've never seen one. In fact, you don't even need a tool *if you know how.* However, a shovel is most commonly used, so I will present that method first.

Karen has found a nice patch and prepares to harvest.

After you've honed your shovel and sited your plot of wild onions (and verified by their smell, for any first timers out there, that they are not some other plant), get on your knees. Some people squat, others bend from the waist.

Brian readies a clump for taking by removing the 'mulch'.

Begin to harvest by clearing away some of the debris of twigs and dead maple leaves in and around a grouping of larger plants. Working a spade halfway under the clump, pry up a bit to loosen the bulbs. Then, start working through the bunch with your fingers to gently separate and pull up the ones you want. It often helps to leave the shovel in place in the event that the clump needs additional loosening. Just watch out that you do not cut your fingers.

Taking only the mature ones.

When you have a handful, make sure that it doesn't include foreign matter other than dirt, that the bulbs are separated (not attached to each other by a common rhizome), and that it is stacked neatly in your hand. Hold them by the upper half, gently so the leaves are not damaged. Now whack the bulbs once on your hand, or on the shovel handle, to remove some of the dirt. Then pack them into a plastic tote or other container. Keep orderly, but rather loose, because you have to unpack them later to wash them.

1/8 lb.; if wholesale priced, 50 cents.

Do this all as quickly as possible if you expect to make the effort worthwhile. By now, you have probably noticed that it takes a while to get a pound.

Sometimes we harvest into pails. They are easier to carry long distances than are totes. Four 5-gallon pails make one full tote.

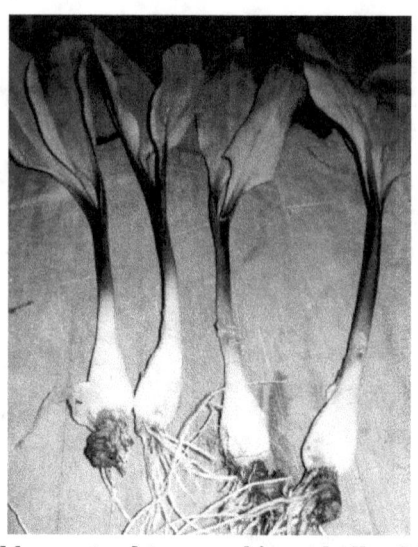

Big broad leaves tend to mean bigger bulbs. Like these!

Feel free to crawl along on your hands and knees as you go from clump to clump dragging your tote and your shovel. Of course, there's more to it than that, and we'll get down and dirty before we're done, but I want to introduce the other method so some comparisons can be made.

In certain circumstances, it is best to forget the shovel. Of all the factors that will affect your ability to do this, the biggest is seasonal, the later the better. In fact, this is the only method you will use in the summer when you are obtaining only the bulbs. Another factor that will allow you to ditch the shovel is soil type. It takes awhile to learn to dig them, and then it takes awhile longer to learn to go without the shovel.

Anyway, you begin much the same, by clearing away the debris of twigs and dead tree leaves in and around your quarry. Then you work your fingers down into the earth deep enough to bend a leek up by its bulb until it breaks free from the rest. If the first one won't give, try another, or two at once, until you succeed.

If you can find an individual leek to 'pop out' of the bunch, you can often get more to follow. The leeks will often come out of the ground cleaner by picking than by digging, and with less root and rhizome, so you may not need to whack them to get the dirt off.

This sometimes faster and easier method of harvesting can pile up the product, so it is tempting to use even when conditions favor the shovel. Be aware that picking them rather than digging may require you to tug a little harder, weakening their stems. You might put up a hundred pounds in a day, but at what cost? Damaged product spoils quickly. At first glance, the ramps look fine. It takes a couple days before the damage becomes obvious—the damaged stem cannot feed the leaf, resulting in a limp leek, which can quickly turn to mush. If you are selling fresh spring leeks, buyers like lush green leaves.

We sell a few summer bulbs at the local 'producer only' farmers' market. They are easy to harvest.

MADE IN THE SHADE

Now then, you have been keeping your container at your side as you work, right? Maybe not.

That is the most efficient way to work because you can put handfuls away as you get them, but if it is sunny out and if you plan to harvest for an hour into the same container, you'll want to keep them in the shade of a nearby tree trunk. An hour in the mid-day sun can reduce your product's ultimate hold-time by as much as a week.

The shade moves faster the farther it is from the tree.

When your container is full, get some cold water on those roots. Karen and I often harvest as a team and so we fill a tote rather quickly. Roots have no chance to get dry this way. However, the single harvester will want to consider a smaller container on warm days, or put water on the roots when the it's half-full. If choosing the latter option, set your tote in the shade while you use another to gather the rest.

Making shade at Joe's ramp camp.

And that's the basics.

FINER POINTS

For this book to reach the most people and to do the most good, it must be aimed at the individual who wants to include ramps, and probably other forgeables in their diet on a regular basis, without guilt. The guilt-free part is easy if you own an acre or two of woods packed with ramps and such. A small family won't need much more than that to keep them forever. Another good place for the non-commercial harvester to gather his fill would be on public lands where ramps are often quite abundant. Many of the morel hunters in our local Manistee National Forest consider leeks a welcome accompaniment to their mushrooms.

If you are harvesting your own little piece of ground for personal use, you have a few less things to think about than the commercial gatherer, most of which are not directly related to the act of harvesting. Those things are covered fully in coming chapters, but I'll touch on some relevant points now.

Karen and I use a lot of onions, and garlic too, more than some folks, less than others. We also use many wild leeks, but all the leeks we eat are a byproduct of our commercial operation. We end up using what we don't send to the distributor or sell at market.

If you harvest only for your family, you can take all you need in a short time, as you need them. So you won't need to pace yourself, or worry about the aches and pains from long hours of the same work. Go as slow or as fast as you want. We know we've been at it too long when we start seeing green on the backs of our eyelids at bedtime.

Brian trying not to fall out of his patch.

The other thing is quality, and it concerns the harvester in two ways: hold times, and cosmetics. You may or may not be particularly concerned with either if they are for 'home use,' but a buyer wants the best of both worlds. The methods I am presenting will work whatever your situation.

Harvesting tools vary. A ramp-digging tool can be made or purchased. A hammer sized hand tool with a long, narrow head works. For commercial purposes a tool that can be used all day, week after week, is essential.

Judging the bulb depth before cutting the roots.

I use a shortened shovel with a serrated edge ground into it. I keep it as sharp as a pocketknife by sharpening it throughout the day with a file. When slicing under a clump with whatever tool you use, you are trying not to slice the bulbs of course. However, you don't want too many roots, so you are trying to guide the edge of your tool through the rhizome. You do this by ear and by touch, and by learning how ramps grow in response to where exactly they are growing (in a cradle, on a knoll, under brush, by a tree etc.).

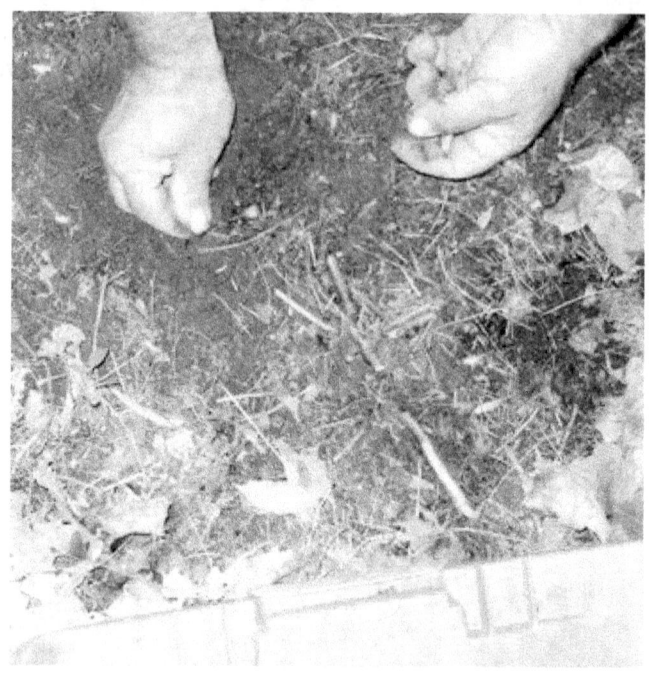

Summer harvesting—by now the leaves are gone, but the bulbs are nice and big. No shovel needed.

PRESERVATION TECHNIQUES

Rarely do we eat them raw, so for our purposes preserved leeks work well for many uses. Canned, pickled, dried or frozen, we have tried all of the above, and each has its place in our bag of culinary tricks.

The versatile ramp will serve you well all year. Like their onion cousins, they preserve well by conventional methods, unlike most onions they don't store well in a root cellar (or I should say, there would be little point, since they live a root cellar life 10 months of the year).

You might wonder, "Why preserve them at all if you can get them anytime that the soil isn't frozen?"

A ramp's talent is not that it goes through roughly all the same things as other perennial forbs and herbs, but the schedule it keeps; they are already out of bed to greet spring's other early risers. They are yellowed and gone when tardier plants are first showing their tender shoulders.

Yes, the bulbs are always there, but they are also always moving from one stage of existence to another. The skin, which can be rather thick in spring, slowly dissolves into the soil as the bulb's outer layer forms a new one.

Like so many things, ramps fill their little niche. And an important niche it is, and like so many things, they live on the edge of existence. By the time spring arrives, bulb and rhizome are shrunken, depleted. In its roots and rhizome, it carries life forward winter after winter. Deep roots pump growth hormones upward in an all-or-nothing try for light.

So, during the course of its seasonal changes, the bulb goes through a few months of desirability followed by a slow decline in palatability.

You'll do right to think about preservation as you harvest and even before. You can't always get to preserving them right away, but that need not matter much. Remember that the advice on keeping quality up during harvest can extend hold-time by as much as 100%, so always think ahead unless you know you are going to preserve or use your haul in a hurry. Hint: for a better product, begin with the freshest (and the biggest).

Refrigeration is a kind of preservation too. While they are available fresh, they will keep in the fridge up to two weeks. Wild leeks should be well wrapped for storage to protect the rest of the contents of the fridge from the aroma.

Note: The green tops are milder in flavor and may be used with or without the bulbs. We add one or two to a sandwich, or chop half a dozen raw leaves into a salad. If however, you have fresh leeks and are only using the bulbs, consider air-drying the leaves—it goes quicker than for the bulbs and you can easily powder them to use as a seasoning. Or chop and freeze the leaves in pint jars for later use.

EFFICIENCY & COSTS

Home food preservation may or may not reduce the cost of food for a family. As the person in charge of operations, you have responsibility for keeping costs low. Luckily, with so many things under your control, you have one opportunity after another to do so.

We feel good about preserving any food though, even if it does sometimes cost a bit more than from the store. There are subsidies and costs associated with store bought items that are not reflected on the price tag. Further, we would never expect to find the same quality there, as we would from home.

In the case of ramps, we wouldn't expect to find them there at all.

The cost of the food that you preserve depends on several factors: the amount you paid for your produce, the cost of your equipment, supplies and fuel, and whether or not you put a dollar value on your time. Preserving seasonal foods when plentiful will result in the greatest savings.

You *can* roughly compare the cost of items you preserve at home with the cost of purchasing similar foods in the store. And yes, you can buy ramps fresh and in various value-added forms. *If you know where to look.* They are not cheap however. And right there the forager has a price advantage preserving his own. So much so, in fact, that I'd bet preserving ramps is done exclusively by those who gather their own.

But for some individuals, preserving food at home may help with a special diet, such as reducing salt or sugar in the foods they eat. In fact many folks have their health in mind when they 'put up' food.

You can get leeks ready for preservation or for immediate consumption by pulling off the outer skin, breaking or slicing off the rhizome and roots, and rinsing until clean. (This is a good way to store them in the fridge so they'll be ready to use as you need them).

All of the preservation methods below begin with clean product and the advice to assemble all of your tools and related items in a clean uncluttered workspace. We like to do as much of it outside as is possible.

VALUE ADDED

You may place a value on your own satisfaction at having directly provided sustenance for your family. You may deem this important enough to offset the value you place on your time.

The methods below will help you estimate the cost of your preserved ramps (or anything else you put in your pantry). You may also have the cost of added ingredients: Determine any items you will need to preserve foods that will add to the cost of the final product. Thus, you can figure your total preservation costs. Or at least get close enough for practical purposes.

If you do need to calculate your costs more accurately, you are probably contemplating marketing some form of processed/packaged product. Value added goods are one way to make money from ramps. Consider an incubator kitchen, which is a professional grade place that you can rent cheaply enough to make a determination as to the profit potential of an idea. They can help you with research, promotional plans, taste tests etc.

To determine the cost of the product, begin by considering the cost of the land, taxes, landowner fees etc. We pay landowners 10% of what we get paid (or if it ends up as home-use,10% of what we would have gotten paid had we sold it). There may be other costs in harvesting; mileage for instance, and time *to some people* is the same as money.

CANNING

I could write a whole chapter on canning leeks. Instead, I will refer you to your Canner Manual and whatever methods you usually use to can onions (alone or as part of something else, like spaghetti sauce or canned meat).

We have used both frozen and dried leeks when canning stewed tomatoes in years when our onion patch produced low. We've put them in canned pizza sauce, salsa and soup. I suppose they would can just as well on their own, just bulbs with water and a pinch of salt. If you try it, let us know.

Best Used For: Anything in which you would use onions. Keep in mind that you use fewer leeks than onions.
Time To Harvest: Spring for leaves. Summer for bulbs.
Type Of Container: Glass only. Size of your choice.
General Method: Again, refer to your own resources. Use as onions (reduce by 1/3 due to their strength).
Storage Time: Indefinite.

PICKLING

Unless you really come to love leeks this way, pint size is probably best although if you open a quart at a party they will often all disappear. People will eat them just so they can't smell them on other people's breath, maybe.

There are many ways to pickle leeks. I'm presenting only the basic operation here. Go online to find more recipes than you could want.

Note: We often end up with a lot of leeks that we can't sell for one reason or another, some minor defect that results in them going to the home-use pile. We end up pickling many of these (bulbs only), but I think I would rather wait to use the summer bulbs instead, for reasons I'll go into below

Best Used For: On the pickle tray at large gatherings. As an occasional appetizer with bread and cheese and wine. Chopped finely into certain salads for a little zing. Sliced into a sandwich. Chopped into sweet and sour dishes.

Time To Harvest: Probably summer. I don't see any point in pickling the leaves, or even the leaf stem except maybe as a handle. So unless you have a good reason to, you may as well not pickle any until after the flower stage. Just don't wait so long that they get tough.

Type Of Container: Glass only. We use quarts and pints. I've heard of folks successfully reusing the jars and lids from store bought pickles, and as long as the lids are in good shape, do as you will.

Tools To Use: Measuring cup and spoons. Knife. Stainless steel 2-quart kettle.

General Method: Clean, remove leaves, pack jars, make brine, fill & seal jars.

Storage Time: Up to a year.

Pickling in detail:

Ingredients—(makes one quart)

1lb ramps bulbs wash and trimmed	¼ C salt
1 ½ C vinegar	1 ½ C water
1 small hot pepper	1 C sugar
2 med. grape leaves	Dash allspice.

1. Pack bulbs, pepper and grape leaves into clean qt. jar.
2. Combine other ingredients in medium saucepan on medium to high heat.
3. Bring to boil, stirring often.
4. Pour hot brine over ramps—fill to ½ inch from top.
5. Cap and cool.

To Determine the Cost of Pickling or Canning

Disregard the cost of the pressure canner, it should have a twenty year life span. Same for your water bath canner at ten years and any other equipment since these expenses should be spread out over hundreds of batches of home canned goods.

DO INCLUDE the cost of jars and screw bands (divided by expected ten year life) since you may only use once yearly. Add the cost of new lids.

Add fuel for preparing and processing (your gas or power company can supply rates for different processes).

Labor?

Storing Canned or Pickled Ramps

Canned products make seasonal produce available all year, until needed, unaffected by power failures. The quality is however affected by the temperature at which they are stored. A general chemical law says that the rate of a natural chemical reaction doubles for each 18-degree rise in temperature (at least within the ranges we are considering).

Canned goods have an indefinite shelf life until opened. Heat during processing inactivates enzymes and drastically slows chemical reaction, but cannot stop them completely. Chemical changes may affect the color, texture taste and/or nutritive value of foods.

Just as warmth tends to have a detrimental effect, so too can extreme cold. Freezing does not make canned food unsafe, *unless* the jar gets cracked or a cap gets loosened, which would let in bacteria. Many canned foods will soften in texture, if frozen.

For the maximum quality and nutrition value follow the storage recommendations below.

1. Test the seal.
2. Remove the screw bands.
3. Wash the jar's outside clean to remove any stickiness, dry thoroughly before storing.
4. Label, contents and year.
5. Check periodically. Beware of any signs of spoilage. Mold, odor, etc…
6. If the seal has broken, DO NOT USE!!

FREEZING

Best Used For: Probably the most useful of all, this technique is quick simple and may be the only one you need.

Leaves or bulbs, it's nice to have some on hand for a quick addition to any number of dishes that call for onion. It doesn't take much cooking to soften them up. Toss into a kettle of simmering soup just before you turn off the heat.

Time to Harvest: If you just want the bulbs you can wait until early summer. Early summer bulbs are bigger, better and easy to get.

Type of Container: Glass, plastic bags or freezer containers.

Note: We have used glass more and more. Breakage is rarely a problem, with care. Using glass has advantages not to be overlooked. We re-use old lids when freezing in jars. One advantage to using glass jars is that you don't need to label the ones that you can identify by sight—same goes for stuff in plastic bags. We don't even date frozen leeks since we know we'll be using them in less than a year.

Ready to rinse.

Tools to Use: Bowls, hose and knives.

General Method: Clean, chop, drain, package and freeze.

Storage Time: 6 to 9 months at 0°F

Other: No need to blanch first.

Freezing In Detail

1. Starting with clean leeks, cut into useable sized pieces. Keep bulb and leaf pieces in separate bowls.

2. Pack separately (you may want to use bulbs and leaves for different things).

3. Close lids securely.

4. Spread containers out at first so they will freeze faster.

Storing Frozen Ramps

Freezing is a technique we learned from nature, and relearned recently in much the same way when a group of hungry explorers discovered a wholly mammoth in a melting glacier, and ate it.

If you own a generator, you don't need to worry about things like losing a freezer full of food in a power outage, like we did a couple years ago when there were no glaciers around. Other than that, there's not much to it.

Packing leaves and bulbs in separate jars.

1. If using plastic bags, store inside another larger sealable bag. If glass jars are put in a chest freezer they should go in a box so they don't get lost, and broken.

Note: Whether bulbs or a pieces, they tend to freeze together a bit. It's normal, but it does keep them from pouring out when you go to use them. We loosen them in the jar by jabbing at them with a paring knife. When they are in plastic bags, we break them apart by whamming the bag on a counter. To cure this problem we might try freezing them on cookie trays before packing.

<u>To Determine the Cost of Freezing</u>

Freezing is said to be the worst choice for long term storage. The cost goes up daily as the quality goes slowly down. We try to use freezer goods in under six months.

Again, because of its lifespan you can ignore the cost of the freezer itself, but not the cartons, bags and/or jars.

For the cost of electricity to maintain 0°F, check with your power company, or estimate at $80 to $125 per year depending on the size and age of your freezer. Divide by the percentage of space a given item fills and multiply by the time spent there.

Labor, again the big question, "what to pay yourself???"

DRYING

Best Used For: Handy to toss into casseroles, soups, stews. Leaves are good powdered and used like powdered onion.

Time to Harvest: Early summer bulbs are as good or better than spring's.

Type Of Container: Quart or pint glass jars, plastic containers, plastic bags.

Tools to Use: Thermometer, cookie sheets, knife (paring), solar or some other dehydrator or oven.

General Method: Clean, chop, spread, dry, turn or rotate, dry more, package and store.

Storage Time: Up to a year.

Other: No need to blanch first. Drying reduces volume by about ½. Rehydrating restores volume to 100%. Keep in mind bulbs may or may not need to be pre-rehydrated when adding to dishes no need to rehydrate separately, especially if the dish you are cooking has a little extra moisture in it and if it's a slow cooking type dish.

Drying in Detail

1. Cut up as for freezing but smaller, making sure that the bulb pieces are no longer than ¼ inch, and keeping leaf and bulb pieces separate.

2. Spread the pieces out in a single layer on trays. Cookie sheets work in the oven but not as well in a solar dryer. In fact, a solar dryer may not be the best choice if using early spring leeks, because the sun may not cooperate. It takes at least 12 hours at 120°F in an oven (We've had it take all of 3 days in the solar unit). If using a commercial dehydrator follow the manufacturer's guidelines for onions.

3. Do not prepare more than you can dry at one time and do not crowd them on the trays.

4. Put an oven thermometer toward the middle of the tray. If using more than one tray, switch them around several times to promote even dehydration.

5. Check more frequently toward end to prevent scorching.

6. Dry until crisp and brittle.

7. To properly condition pieces after initial drying pour them into a deep container, cover w/cheese cloth for a couple days. Stir twice daily.

8. To store, pack into airtight containers or double plastic bags. Do not pack containers tightly

Storing Dried Ramps

Dehydration is another technique learned untold ages ago from nature—our first experience with dried food would have been accidental. However, us being human, it wouldn't take us long to improve on the whole operation. Truly dry foods in airtight containers (or pyramids) can last for centuries. As with canned foods, you can't stop all enzymatic and chemical processes, but you can keep them to a minimum. Unlike canned foods, freezing dried goods will not affect them.

1. Label if you need to.
2. Keep packed loosely in airtight containers sealed tightly.
3. Store in a cool, dry dark place.
4. Use for as long as they last. Humidity over time can tend to make them stale.
5. If seal has been broken, inspect for mold—if none, go ahead and use.

To rehydrate, put in pan or bowl. Add enough water to cover, and let stand until soft (half an hour +/-). (May be cooked in their soaking water until tender or added to another dish that is cooking.)

To Determine the Cost of Drying

Nil if you use a solar dehydrator—but probably two to four dollars per batch with gas or electric, depending on the batch size. We have a couple electric dehydrators but we rarely use them since it is so much more economical to use solar. Sometimes the sun cooperates with this plan, other times we use gas or electricity to dry part or all of a batch.

Labor? Give yourself a raise for showing up early. 10% more of nothing is still nothing.

Note; There are no further costs, even to rehydrate foods, since normal cooking times should suffice.

HOME COOKING TO HIGH CUISINE

"Until shortly after the turn of the 20th century, many American cooks relied on foods they either raised themselves or foraged from the land to feed their families. An intimate knowledge of nature provided these self-sufficient cooks with the makings of wholesome meals. With an increase in industrialization, however, came greater dependency on food manufacturers and neighborhood markets—and the conveniences they provide. Eventually, we grew accustomed to the ease of filling our pantries and freezers with boxed and canned goods, distancing our connection with the land that yielded them." Joanne L. Hayes, The Wild Things

If you like to cook with fresh foods, April is a challenging month for the best cooks. While we are waiting for our gardens to catch up, and those remaining fruits and roots stored from last season's harvest are dwindling, it's only natural to turn to wild edibles. You don't even need a recipe to enjoy them. Ramps make a fine accompaniment to almost any meal boiled alone, salted and buttered.

Ramps are valued for their distinct flavor, which enhances the flavor of other ingredients in any dish; and they are particularly good cooked with bland, starchy foods like legumes or potatoes. (Cooking takes much of the curative value out of ramps!). We put the fresh leaves on our sandwiches when we take a break from harvesting.

Our experience substituting wild leeks for onions and garlic has lead to some surprises: it doesn't work well in every case. First it's the intensity of the flavor, which can be cooked down a bit by adding them earlier in the cooking process, or reduced by adjusting down the amount (to suit your tongue). Second, it's the quality of the flavor. *It's wild.* Compared to onions, it's like venison is to beef, like brookies to tilapia. And if garlic is the Stinking Rose, ramps are the King of Stink according to one devoted web site. (The word stink in relation to both of these old plants would be in the olden vernacular of course, where the word stinken just meant a strong odor, good or bad. Right?)

There are many species of Allium, a genus of the Lily family; The most popular of which is the garden variety onion, probably native to western Asia, as it is mentioned in old Egyptian writings and in the Pentateuch (first five books of the Bible). The onion has spread to all countries occupied by man.

There are slightly less than an infinite number of recipes calling for onions, scallions, garlic, and/or garden leeks. Some of these work well enough when you interchange ingredients amongst the allium family, and that includes the various wild varieties found around the world. Since there is already a cookbook devoted to ramps, and umpteen dozen recipes on-line, prudence suggests that I pick a few of my favorites for inclusion here.

Cooks have for hundreds of years relied upon the Alliums to bring out the best in their most cherished recipes. As a bonus, onions and their kin are a valuable source of important minerals, calcium, phosphorus and iron. Leeks contain protein, vitamin C, and sulfur, and are low in sodium. Giant cousin to the wild ramp, garden variety leeks were once the staple vegetable of Europe. In recent years, they have made something of a comeback. The garden leek is slightly milder in flavor than the common yellow onion (which makes it a welcome addition to any food from soup to salad). Different varieties of onions range from sweet and mild to pungent and spicy. Common chives are the mildest alliums of all. And who is strongest?

Others may disagree, but I put ramps right below garlic. Real garlic that is, not elephant garlic. While elephant garlic is actually a leek, it produces very large, garlic-like cloves with a mild garlic flavor (though the taste sharpens in cold winter climates). Bulbs commonly weigh up to one pound each.

I say, "Use them all."—and I do.

Ramps and breaded potato wedges ready to bake.

"On the other hand, certain yogic diets prohibit the onion because it is said to 'increase body heat and the appetites.' This may be because the onion acts as a stimulant to the adrenal glands. Those with weak adrenal glands should eat of the onion family sparingly as should individuals sensitive to sulfur-containing foods." From Nourishing Traditions by Sally Fallon

TEN WAYS WITH RAMPS

WILD LEEK PIE Makes dinner for four when served with fresh greens and a fruit salad.

Pastry shell	2 C half & half
4 med. eggs	1 ½ t of salt
½ C grated sharp cheddar cheese	1/8 t of nutmeg
25-30 med. leek bulbs and petioles	
5-6 bacon slices	

Line a pie pan with your favorite pastry, brush the shell with a little beaten egg, and bake it for five minutes in a 425°F oven. Meanwhile, steam the bulbs for about 8 minutes, then drain. Place the bulbs in the crust, and add bacon.

Mix the rest of the beaten egg with half & half, salt and nutmeg. Pour mixture over bacon and leeks, and put the pan into a 350°F oven for 10 minutes before turning down to 325°F (continue to bake until filling has set (20 minutes or more). Cover with cheese upon removing from oven.

PHEASANT WITH RAMPS & MORELS   Serves 2-4

1 ¼ to 2 ¼ lb ready-to-roast pheasant, split in half
12 medium Ramps (bulbs and leaves)
1 T melted butter
½ t salt
1/8 t ground black pepper
10 fresh morels
2 t fresh or ½ teaspoon dried thyme leaves
½ C dry white wine
Fresh thyme sprigs with flowers (optional)

Pre-heat oven to 350°F. Rinse pheasant and pat dry. Remove any excess fat from body and neck cavities. Thoroughly rinse ramps and pat dry—cut bulbs from leaves. Slice leaves lengthwise; set aside. Place bulbs in 8-inch baking pan. Place pheasant halves, skin sides up, on top of bulbs. Brush with melted butter; sprinkle with salt and pepper.

Roast 45 to 50 minutes or until fork-tender. Remove bulbs and pheasant from baking pan to two plates; keep warm.

Meanwhile, in a small skillet, combine mushrooms and thyme with drippings from baking pan. Sauté until mushrooms soften—3 to 5 minutes. Stir white wine and ramp leaves into mushroom mixture; cook 3 to 5 minutes.

With slotted spoon, remove mushroom mixture to plates with pheasant. Serve excess liquid as sauce with pheasant. Garnish with thyme sprigs, if desired.

Variations: Other small birds work well, as do other wild mushrooms.

ZESTY PESTO

Extra-virgin olive oil
Wild oregano
Ramps, with or without leaves

Process plants in equal quantities with enough oil to make a paste.
For convenience sake, freeze in ice cube trays and bag up.

Variations: Try adding parsley or basil.

BAKED ASPARAGUS & RAMPS   Serves 4

1 lb fresh asparagus
1 lb fresh spring ramps
2 T butter
1 T olive oil
1 T balsamic vinegar

Cut off and discard the top 1/3 of the ramp leaves. Drizzle olive oil on a cookie sheet—roll whole ramps and asparagus in it and spread out. Bake at 350°F for 15-20 minutes or until tender. Melt butter, add balsamic vinegar, stir, and drizzle over baked spears or use as a dipping sauce.

For a great variation on this recipe: Cook on the grill—baste with butter, oil and vinegar while grilling. And if there's room on the grill for your entree, you can avoid using the cook stove altogether.

ROOT ROAST   Serves 4-6

2 ½-3 lbs mixed vegetables: potatoes, carrots, ramp bulbs, turnips, parsnips and sweet potatoes. (Vary amounts, add or substitute other root crops as you wish.)
Several short rosemary sprigs or 10 sage leaves
3 bay leaves
Olive oil
Salt & freshly milled pepper

Peel and/or clean the vegetables. Preheat oven to 450°F. Cut everything into pieces roughly the same size except for the parsnips, sweet potatoes, and turnips, which cook faster and can be slightly larger than the rest.

Toss the vegetables and herbs with oil to coat lightly, then season with salt and pepper. Put everything in a roomy pan. Bake uncovered in the top third of the oven 20 minutes, shaking once or twice.

Reduce heat to 375°F and continue baking until the vegetables are tender when pierced with a knife, 20 - 30 minutes. Remove the bay leaves. Sprinkle herb salts or vinegar over the vegetables as soon as they come out of the oven.

By the way: Bulbs are bulbs, not roots. Rutabagas, turnips, radishes etc. are the true root crops. If we get it underground we tend to call it a root, but just as a potato's tubers are actually part of the stem of the plant, onion bulbs are actually leaf parts. It is the rhizome, not the bulb, which grows the roots.

DANDELION & WILD ONION SALAD   Serves 2
One handful each, dandelion & ramp leaves

Gather the white crown and very small green leaves of dandelions—use whole. Chop ramp leaves into small pieces and toss them with the dandelion crowns.

Variations: If you've got some salad greens going in a cold frame by the time the dandelions and leeks are up—add them to this salad in equal parts with the others. Add two slices crumbled bacon.

Note: The dandelion is delicious, tender and mild when still a white crown growing just below the surface of the ground. Even a few flowers appearing in a field of dandelions indicate that all of the greens growing in that area will taste bitter. However, since they are so incredibly nutritious, it is worth finding a way to mask the bitterness so that you may enjoy the benefits. This salad is a real energy booster. Both plants provide many vitamins and minerals when we need them most.

Dressing for Dandelion and Wild Onion Salad:

½ t salt	1 C skim milk
3 T all-purpose flour	2 T sugar
1/8 t ground black pepper	3 T cider vinegar

In 1-quart saucepan, combine milk, flour, sugar, salt & pepper. Cook over medium heat, stirring until mixture thickens—3 to 5 minutes. Remove from heat and stir in vinegar. Use dressing hot or cold.

VEGETABLE RAMP MEDLEY   Serves 5-6

2 C chopped ramp bulbs
2 C chopped zucchini
2 C chopped carrots
1 red pepper chopped
4 T butter
Sea salt & pepper to taste

Vegetables should be cut into uniform pieces. Cutting can be done hours in advance. Cut off and discard ends of zucchini, remove inner parts, chop, and set aside. Seed the pepper and cut into, 1-inchsquares—set aside.

Cut carrots and ramps—sauté in butter. When they are just tender, add the pepper and cook about 1 minute. Add zucchini and sauté another minute. Season to taste.

GLAZED RAMPS   Serves 4-5

36 to 48 ramp bulbs
7 C boiling water
2 t salt
4 t butter (melted)
3 t sugar

Cook bulbs uncovered in boiling water to which 1½ t salt has been added, for 15 minutes. Drain. Put in baking dish.

Mix melted butter, sugar and remaining ½ t salt together, pour over ramps. Bake uncovered at 350°F for 25 minutes, or until glazed and lightly browned.

CREAM OF WILD ONION SOUP — Serves 3-4

2 ½ C milk
3 C thinly sliced ramps
3 T butter
½ t dry mustard
1 t salt
2 T flour
Nutmeg freshly grated
White pepper

Optional extra seasonings:
Worcestershire sauce
Cayenne pepper

Toppings:
½ t prepared horseradish
Croutons
Finely minced pimiento

Heat milk slowly in heavy saucepan (lowest heat) until it just reaches the boiling point. Turn off heat. This is known as scalding the milk. (Don't cool the milk before proceeding.)

In another saucepan, cook the ramps with salt and mustard, in butter over low heat, until they are very limp and soft, but not brown. Sprinkle the flour into the ramps, mixing with a spoon as you sprinkle. Stir and cook the mixture another 3-4 minutes over medium-low heat.

Add the scalded milk, stir well, cover and cook another 10-15 minutes over lowest possible heat (use a heat absorption pad underneath, if you have one). Stir it from the bottom every few minutes. It will become thick and creamy.

Add a few dashes of white pepper, nutmeg and optional seasonings, to taste. Serve topped with croutons and/or minced pimiento.

RAMSON SOUP   Serves 6

4 C ramp bulbs
4 T butter
2 Qt beef stock
½ C cognac
½ C red wine
2 T arrowroot powder mixed with 2 T water
Salt & pepper

Chop ramps thinly. Melt butter in a large, stainless steel pot. Add ramps and cook on the lowest possible heat, stirring occasionally, for up to an hour, or until they are soft and slightly caramelized. Raise heat a bit and cook a few minutes, stirring constantly. The ramps should turn brown but not burn.

Add wine, cognac and stock. Bring to a rapid boil and skim off any foam that may rise to the top. Add the arrowroot mixture to thicken, stir and season to taste. Serve with round croutons and a platter of cheeses.

Variation: Use ½ cup armognac instead of cognac.

OUR STORY—GREEN GOLD?

Another spring draws near, another leek season. The harvest and sale of hundreds of pounds of fresh spring leeks has taken on such an importance for us that we have arranged for a month each year to focus on little else. We run a small wildcrafting business called Found in The Woods.

THE TWO SIDES OF FOUND IN THE WOODS

On one hand, we produce and provide a unique list of top-quality goods. On the other, we offer a range of specialized skills for hire.

Wildcrafting, or harvesting non-timber forest products, is the broad term for much of what we market; nature's craft supplies and curiosities, firewood, wild foods and the medicinal herbs of the upland forests. We also provide a range of related services; tree-work (from transplanting to first aid, to problem removal), landscaping and *waterscaping*, green construction and more.

Osceola County

LeRoy Township

RAISE YOUR RIGHT HAND, "WE ARE HERE."

We *are* often found in the woods. Michigan's forests provide us a modest living. Some of the goods we deal in come from our own property, especially the plants and produce we grow for the local farmers' market—more we hope, as time goes on. Even if we get the product from 200 miles away, it comes home with us for some sort of after-harvest processing.

Michigan has had a long and important role in supplying forest products of all kinds. The Upper Peninsula alone was a major source of natural resources that helped fuel territorial expansion and economic development of the United States.

We consider our family's property a good example of the Lower Peninsula's finest country. Some of our services, such as lessons and classes, are performed here too. Our property is part of Michigan's upland, a unique sort of borderland. This glacially sculpted country stretches east and west in a narrow band across the 'mitten' from Manistee on Lake Michigan to Tawas City on Lake Huron. Here we enjoy a nice compromise between the two vastly different environs found to the north and south.

Like our neighbors far and wide, we deal with a legacy of the settler mindset. What they saw as pioneering and raising a family *bless their hearts* resulted in a net-loss for the land. We live with less topsoil and less biodiversity— more non-native invasive species and more pollution in general. However, on my family's land, the forest has been taking it back. Mostly thanks to the forethought and stewardship of our parents, Melvin "Mike" and Norma Cool.

Dad is gone now, but his love for the outdoors is kept alive in the hearts of his eight kids, and in the land we share in trust. Our family is blessed to own one of the most diverse acreages around these parts. The original homestead has been in the Cool name since 1910. We call it Cool Acres as you might guess. It now encompasses nearly 250 acres.

LIFE AT THE GREEN POLE

Green Pole? Like the South Pole? Not quite . . . it's the name of our house and home. (We based the design upon the Earthwood house built by Rob and Jaki Roy). It is also home to the business office of Found in The Woods. But what does the name mean? Well, it's hard to put into words, especially since the place . . . named itself.

Our house is a sampler of the alternative field of 'green building'. It is a circular two-story structure built into a south facing hillside, handcrafted from wood off our own property. We've included such principles as mortgage free, integrative design *or permaculture*, scavenging materials, build-with-what-you-have, and option based thinking.

Design features include, a passive solar-loop, 50% earth sheltered, thermal mass, composting toilets and a grey water treatment system. Specific building styles include a sod roof, rock masonry, curved cordwood walls, straw-bale walls, surface bonded block and rustic post and beam.

Our home in the woods, the Green Pole.

Foragers tend to be do-it-yourselfers so it won't surprise you that the Green Pole was built almost entirely by Karen and me. *Not that it went up quick.* Our forager mentality also shines through in our choice to gather cast-offs and leftover building materials locally. All the glass for windows, all the rubber for roofing, all the re-rod for floor and footing, all the fixtures and wire for our 12-volt electric system, more than a thousand cement blocks and much more were scrounged. People were as happy to get rid of stuff as we were to have it.

All of these building, business and lifestyle choices are just part of our attempt to approach a state of balance with nature. How will we ever know we have arrived?

Only a fool would answer that.

Maybe it's the journey that counts, in the end.

Karen and I regularly include wild foods in our diet from numerous sources; lake and marsh, field and forest, and anything in between. Do we do it to keep our food bills down? To keep life interesting? For our health? Do we do it just because we know how?

We forage because it feels right, and tastes right. (We happen to be good enough at it to sell some). Wild foods, including game, make up about 15-20% of our diet. Most of the rest comes from the garden, goats or chickens.

We began business in 2003. Starting Found in The Woods was the culmination of a lifetime dream for us. We wanted to live and work the way in which most of our ancestors must have, close to the Earth and in step with the seasons. We feel fortunate to be doing something we love. Much of our business and management history ties in with our previous partnership, the popular ski destination 'Cool's Cross Country Farm' 1994-2002.

FiTW is built around these principles:
Fair prices for excellent products and services
Supporting the interests of our customers
Maintaining a deep connection to Nature

These values support each other as we uphold them—the fair and friendly service we provide is largely a result of this reciprocal relationship. When we work for sustainability, we get so much more in return. Earth's fragile web of life deserves more respect that we can give. Not because it's a trendy marketing tool, the places we have worked are some small proof that our methods matter. In addition, the landowners we work with keep letting us back.

SO THAT WE MAY ALSO LEARN

Foraging comes natural to us humans, but some education in the finer points is worthwhile. In olden days, when a Paleo-diet was the rule, such education came young.

Nowadays, I read about the occasional effort to literally and totally live-off-the-land, for a period of time or for a day each week. Setting goals like that is fine, though probably many fall short of their goal—but better that than never to try. It gets easier if you keep learning new varieties of wild edibles and new methods to harvest, preserve and prepare them.

This guidebook seeks to inspire an interest in and a respect for a whole spectrum of forgeables, because in looking for one thing you may find another.

We keep track of when and where to find our favorites, then we make the time to go look. Never a week passes without some forest mushroom in our diet, never a week without some wayside herb in our tea, never a week without wild leeks. We have been eating off the land for decades and selling ramps for years. Recently we've been working toward other options—teaching, farmers' market sales, and publications.

Karen and I have given some informational workshops over the years, mostly to do with cross-country skiing; we've also done food related demonstrations at the LeRoy Farmers' Market, and a 'Green Building Techniques' workshop at our house. So, it seems right to teach foraging too. We did our first Walk/Talk last fall, 2012. We have another scheduled this spring. Leeks will be prominent on the menu for any such foraging presentation, not just because they are such a treat to eat but because they are available almost year-round, if you know where.

Another topic on the menu at any classes we host is sustainability. These day's it is crucial. It's just a matter of learning our place in space.

It is encouraging that people will attend a class on foraging, and I'd help out even if just for the chance to get folks out to commune with the planet. It's also nice to know that you are passing along an age old skill that will enrich someone's life in some practical way.

Still, It's a wonder to us that man has come away so far from the woods that someone should even need such a thing as an edible and medicinal plant workshop. More a wonder that it should be us to facilitate, when the two of us know so little in comparison to almost any of our 'primitive' ancestors. Oh the things our species has learned, only to have collectively forgotten!

I hope and believe that there are new people every day who are reclaiming their right to affirm an age-old bond with nature. Foraging can play a role in this. There are fresh ways to help people learn, and innovative movements to encourage us.

At the first class we 'taught', we learned as much as the students did. We learned about catmint as bug repellent. We also learned to add power lines to our list of suspicious areas. We acknowledged that we need to keep expanding our list of known plants; be able to identify them, and recite their properties and uses.

We also have to remember that what we don't know about plants, will always outweigh what we do.

Phillip and Elizabeth, our two oldest grandkids, learned the basic harvesting method in minutes.

RAMP IT UP

For those who want to take it to another level, the potential for cash income is good for many of the forest's gifts, but for ramps, it's downright profitable. Here the object is the spring leek in all its fresh green glory, and it takes many tons to fill the demand.

NTFPs share an important tradition *near* worldwide. Resources from the forest remain central to many subsistence and local economies of the developing world. The image of the gatherer has been romanticized in the arts as an icon of nature, and recognized by history for their anonymous contributions as civilization builders.

A likeness of the Green Man, another icon of nature, greeted us one morning when we arrived at work.

Beyond meeting the basic needs of health and nutrition for many, NTFPs are a rapidly growing market sector, nationally and internationally. And the market is growing yearly as much as 20%. Development offers income potential and opportunities in rural areas.

Our own experience has shown that even though wildcrafting is done in the niche markets the prospects are good for profits. Much of what we do now, grew from what we'd been doing *as they say* under the table, before we really had a name or a number for the business. It was diggin' leeks that allowed us to make a go of it officially.

Not that it's ever been easy, but that's just life.

Many things go into a successful ramp enterprise. The work can be hard and the hours long, the weather tricky and the season short. You've got to locate leeks and negotiate with landowners, find buyers, clean the harvest, make deliveries and keep the paperwork straight. Now, we've got to do it all sustainably or work ourselves out of a job. And then the hardest part, choosing wisely how to spend all that money.

BY THE WAY OF THE WILDCRAFTER

2003 was our first year of harvesting leeks for cash. We got in at the end of the season. Karen worked a couple days, and I for almost a week, but we made $750. Even as beginners, it was easy for us to see the income potential.

For a number of years prior, Joe had been looking for new areas. He'd been working woods a hundred miles south of us early in the season, also a 30-acre woods 70 miles southeast of here, and then traveling about 25 miles north of here to end the season.

A mutual friend told Joe that leeks grew here on our family farm, so he contacted us and offered us the standard landowner fee of 10% if we would let him harvest. He also said that if someone in the family wanted to get involved, he would show us how. I got the go-ahead from the family. Joe taught us the business and offered to partner up with us for the next season.

As I write this, it is in fact only weeks away from the time when the first ramps will expectantly poke green spears up through the forest floor. We should be harvesting by early to mid-April. Joe, us and the rest of the collection crew will be gathering history. There may be as many as a dozen of us working in loose connection during the season.

We are but a small percentage of those involved in just the harvest of ramps. And ramps are a small percentage of wildcrafting worldwide.

What may seem like a "new" opportunity to many may in fact be one of the original sources of food, fiber, medicine etc. that has sustained humans through the ages. Even in the US and other industrialized countries, they continue to provide important resources for many.

The livelihood strategies of many people in rural and forest communities tend to reflect a connection to natural cycles. Those folks that are drawn to some aspect of wildcrafting are as varied as the products they work with. One trait shared by many of us is that we can simultaneously and sequentially pursue a number of strategies to fill our needs. I'm hoping that just happens to be a general trait of all successful people and not ADHD, e. g.

Non-timber forest products contribute to gatherer's livelihoods in ways both commercial and personal. Edibles are consumed directly as valued and important parts of a gatherer's diet. Medicinal, are used by some to treat minor ailments' in themselves and in family members. Ceremonials are important for traditional cultural practices. Floral and craft materials add beauty to people's lives and are often given as gifts.

Earnings from market uses are often less than the income from a minimum wage job, when time and expenses are factored. Still, such contributions to individual and household livelihoods are often important in other ways. NTFP's have long provided a variety of valued resources to those who deal in them and will continue to do so.

One of the intangible values of wildcrafting is the relative ease with which a knowledgeable person can turn to it in times of need. This is one reason that so many people have wildcrafted something at some point in their lives.

WORKING NATURE'S PLAYGROUND

During what we call the Spring Rush we are out harvesting the luscious wild spring edibles. This lasts from shortly after the spring equinox until just before the summer solstice.

During summer months, we cut firewood and take on building projects and odd jobs. We tend our vegetable patch (much of which goes to the LeRoy Farmers' Market). By the time our local market opens it's too late for spring leeks, but we do sell the summer bulbs there.

Autumn finds us wrapping-up projects, harvesting apples, black walnuts, pine boughs, herbs for tea and medicinal preparations, grapes, mushrooms and much more.

In winter our work takes us through a wonderland of snow-covered evergreens, into deep frozen swamps, over open meadows and windswept hills. This is also when we plan for the coming year, study, work in the shop, sell firewood and start seedlings.

One of the beautiful places we can be found in the spring.

We schedule wildcrafting classes whenever we can. We teach when and where to find wild edibles and herbs, how to harvest sustainably and what to do with the yield. *Go foraging on an empty stomach, it's not like shopping.* We will even travel to do an event away from home. Such events are a good chance to meet new people. Foraging is a communal activity, good for strengthening bonds of friendship and family. We love to take our grandchildren to the woods whenever we can, but I think they may love it more. We can hardly wait to get them into the business.

Many of our services overlap by design, so that people will find us helpful in many ways. Wherever we are, whatever we're doing, we take nature with us, never trying to subdue her, always mindful of what she gives to our spirit.

MAKING IT PAY

If you treat your ramps right you can get top dollar for them. If you work hard, you can make thousands. It is not a job for everyone though. Some folks never quite get up to speed, although they enjoy the experience. Quality is as important as speed though, so as long as you can gather enough to make it worth your while, go for it.

Our system for processing ramps can be broken down into parts that came together from the ideas of various people. The basic operation is easy to learn and easy to modify for different situations. It also compliments our other seasonal activities and products.

If only it wasn't all over so quick. We always try to squeeze one more week out of the season by starting earlier, or going further north at the end. *If a person could harvest spring ramps 6 months a year, they wouldn't have to work the other six.*

OUR WAY HOME

Running a business from home has many advantages . . . and disadvantages (and considerations that are neither). Taxes differ from one situation to another, as do local codes. When business is largely conducted from your home office, yard or garage, your neighbors have a right to expect that your actions will not infringe upon their lives and property. Our township-zoning ordinance designates FiTW as a home occupation, a permitted use. Such classification reflects the low-key nature of wildcrafting.

We make only rare at-home sales. It's unlikely that we could set up a retail outlet at our home for our products.

Our place is really rather remote. For us to sell most of what we harvest, we have to transport it somewhere.

Found in The Woods: It is a description that covers most of the products we sell, and it is a good description of where we will be on any given day. A walk in the woods provides the brain with the perfect mix of stimuli. The more you learn about the woods the more there is to feed your mind and body. We are constantly on the lookout for new things to add to our business' offerings and to our understanding of wilderness.

Such understanding tempers an impulse to focus on profits. It is why we practice sustainability. It reflects a dedication to our chosen trade.

PRODUCTS AND BY-PRODUCTS

You won't find the same assortment of goods anywhere else. Some of our items are protected in the wild, so we have to grow them. Some of our items are found in the oddest of places. Some are only seasonally available. Others are offered only through us. *Like our all-natural wreaths.* Many of the products we offer are sold at the local farmers market, or from home. Except leeks—those we deliver.

We only sell it if we know it. We have sold all of the following wild seasonal items besides leeks, fiddleheads, cattails, nettles, mushrooms, medicinal herbs and craft supply items like ostrich fern spore fronds and pinecones, and finished crafts such as holiday greenery and canes.

As for appearance, we keep the 'scratch and dent' or 'cosmetically challenged' items for our own consumption since we know they are just as good, as long as we use them right away. Using the product also deepens our understanding of it.

MARKETING AND SALES

How we market our various products and services to make a profit means learning about potential customers, their buying habits, and how we will attract and hold them.

Basic marketing plans are prepared as new businesses are being developed. Thereafter, marketing decisions will be made and modified from day to day and from product to product. Two decisions form the basis of our own marketing strategy; a *target market* must be identified, and a *marketing mix* must be developed.

The *target market* is the customers to be served. The *marketing mix* is the combination of a particular product, or service, price, place and promotion to be used in meeting the needs of the identified target market.

For ramps, our target market is a wild food distributor. They purchase our bulk product and resell it in smaller quantities. We could 'move up the food chain' by doing the distributing ourselves if we had the connections, the time, the knowhow and the sales mojo.

Marketing is not just sales efforts, promotional plans, and out-pricing the competition. To us, marketing is building relationships with our customers. Marketing is keeping the 'anchor' in your voice. It is also offering your name and business name when introducing yourself and passing a business card if appropriate.

Marketing 'in the niches' gives a certain pride of individuality on one hand, but on the other, it means being incredibly dedicated.

Marketing is in creating a logo that fits your business.

When we got started, a careful analysis showed a demand for exceptional quality and service in the wild-crafting industry. Over time, we have built our reputation and secured our fair portion of 'the market'. With careful promotion, an eye for opportunities, and good management, we hope to continue to see growth for years to come.

Planning involves examining our past activities and thinking about future activities by forecasting. We should be concerned with such factors as customer preferences, current buying trends, past sales, budgets, product lines, purchases, and pricing. Sales forecasting is a framework upon which many other aspects of planning are hung.

Consideration of conditions outside the business that affect past, present and future sales, are as important as conditions within the business that affect sales.

With any early-season plant there is always the cold to fear. With ramps, the cold is an almost constant companion. You learn to work with it. You have to stay in good health for it, because you don't want to miss a day digging. Too much cold damages the leaves. This is just one of many outside factors that the ramp harvester encounters.

With NMGs, we are applying a number of promotional plans to some very different things! We find it best to have a separate file for each of our different items or services. Many of these files contain individual promotion plans, which compliment the overall marketing plan.

Advertizing is usually based on estimated sales, but it is not true that sales will always be in direct proportion to advertising dollars spent. This can prove to be especially NOT true with most of the NMGs. For a business like ours that has several unique customer groups, a changing marketing mix, or uses several media methods, it *can* be quite complicated.

We don't do any traditional advertising. NMG buyers are found by seeking them out—or they find you if they can. We keep a list of Chambers of Commerce for generating business leads. We do an online catalog brochure of sorts, and distribute various info sheets.

COMPETITIVE EVALUATION

Your best competition is just like you, only better—an honest competitive analysis will evaluate their strengths and weaknesses compared to your own, and suggest necessary adjustments. If your present objectives are not in line with current trends they will be easily recognized by a competitive evaluation. Look at what others are doing to 'stay ahead of the game'.

Take a close look at the barriers or conditions hindering your competitor's physical size or available resources, compared to your own assets *or* other competitor's assets. Then focus on alternative options for performance to remain competitive and flexible. The path to achievement is never obvious, never quite the same for any two people. You may find success by offering more or better choices, or by being recognized as a leader in service, or by any of a number of other choices.

The economic environment also needs to be monitored closely, because of many NMGs being a luxury, which in hard times is the first thing to be eliminated by individuals and families. By adapting to changes, and following marketing strategies, you will have the best chance to be successful.

If it doesn't complicate things unduly, a cheaper or easier or more efficient way of doing things is worth doing. For instance, if a buyer wanted to meet us at home, that would be worth a discount because it saves us delivery charges. Consider such decisions wisely, and be clear about details, so you won't regret having committed to a lose-lose situation. The double-edged sword of business sensibility, while cutting corners, can also cut into profits by unintentionally cheapening the whole operation.

RECORDS & PAPERWORK

Your level of activity in wildcrafting may be such that you need to keep track of the things that won't fit in your head. FiTW depends heavily on the use of a good computer. Before you adopt the use of any program or system, consider it carefully. Let your paperwork serve you.

The paperwork to keep track of a multi-person operation can be made much easier by the creation of a log-sheet tailored to your needs. We use a variety of forms to keep track of different aspects of our wildcrafting business.

Our Ramp Delivery Log shows who does what and how the money is divided.

Our present system is built around the following parameters; 500 acres, 8 workers (including us), 4 weeks work, 2 tons product (approx), 400 lbs of ice roughly, 2000+ miles road time, and several thousand gallons of rinse water. We use one form to keep track of almost everything we do for each delivery. Some of the workers perform only one type of task, like delivery or rinsing, others may do every aspect short of the business details.

We didn't start out using a comprehensive form though. It took many interwoven decisions to hone down four different forms into one. However, with it, we have achieved our original purpose, a simple, full and open accounting of the totals for every load.

The log sheet records the delivery date, time, location, buyer and driver. Each harvester has a section for recording any expenses they may have for their products: ice, landowner fees, rinsing fees etc. Another section logs the cleaner's activities and pay. A final section is for calculating the delivery charges due the driver.

Another bit of paperwork you might be interested in if you live near public property—permits for cutting firewood on state and federal lands. They cost $20 each and you can cut 20 ricks of wood. This will put you in the woods where you might find mushrooms or leeks, which you might then sell at your local farmers' market.

LAND OWNER CONSIDERATIONS

"The briars are steadily pushing their way into every corner of your woods and will soon push us out."

"We had several good days in your woods. I hope you didn't notice we were there. It's our goal to leave your place looking like we found it, and to leave enough leeks to allow small yearly harvests."

"We are willing to pay you a higher percentage for several reasons; your wood's larger acreage, water onsite, it's adjacent to another of our landowners and close to home. It's not the biggest field we harvest, but almost when you add Zimmerman's next door. Having the creek saves us hauling our 15-gallon water barrel."

"Most of our time this year was spent in our southernmost and northernmost areas. We would have liked to work closer to home of course, but the product was damaged early on by sleet and it never quite recovered around here. There are still places in your woods that we've never harvested from. We tried Evart, Reed City, Ashton, LeRoy, and Tustin and finally found good leeks again north of Cadillac. Those big leeks we had to pass up will be even bigger next year."

Excerpts from letters sent to landowners with their checks.

The crew we put together each year could decimate a single location in a short time. I've seen such places . . . where wholesale harvests by migrant workers had left a barren landscape. I've seen spots on federal land where inexperienced or lazy harvesters had left an area looking as if someone had roto-tilled. That is NOT something I'd allow on land that I own. Wait, I do own that, as a US citizen.

I've worked the public lands myself on the rare occasion. We scale our operation down when we harvest in state or federal forests because other harvesters may have been there too, and because we want to be welcomed. We've met and talked with a couple of the foresters we've seen while we were working. One of them spent half a day in the same area . . . us digging ramps, him marking and measuring trees for a timber cut. He saw no harm in what we were doing (harvesting in the midst of hundreds of thousands of plants). He judged our impact to be less than that of the dozens of mushroomers camped nearby.

Sometimes a wood will be slated for clear-cutting or for development, and then it would be best to dig up all the leeks first. Only then. Otherwise, the goal should be to go forth and multiply them.

One reason we seldom harvest from public lands is because of those who do and do it badly. The actions of one careless harvester can influence the opinions of dozens of other people who use and love our public lands. Opinion will often fuel decisions as much as fact. When regulations are finally considered for taking leeks from state and federal lands, it will be because of the actions of a few reckless entrepreneurs. Conversely, those who are willing to meet sustainability requirements, should be allowed to do so.

Found in The Woods has connections with ten to a dozen different locations for ramps each year. Some are through land managers. Most are with private landowners. We pay a percentage of our 'net' for however many pounds we sell from their woods. Find landowners through ads in the paper or word-of-mouth. Line up enough acreage so that you don't deplete your source.

We try to work in a progression from one property to another, based on when the leeks will be best (depending on several factors). South to north would be the general progression, except here in the Great Lakes region where zigzagging between shoreline regions and inland areas seems to work best.

When working a parcel, we begin by communicating with the other gatherers about the area—each property has its own considerations. We also try to work systematically, each worker claiming an area. It is tempting to cover a wood twice in a season, but not generally advisable unless the overall annual harvest is still less than 5%.

Finally, quality begins with the gatherer. We don't harvest, what we can't sell—better to leave them in the ground. Leaves should have no holes, cuts, bruises or bite marks. Leaves should be a lustrous green, no spots, streaks or yellow tips. Bulbs should be whole. Stems should not be stretched or broken. Of course, a few cosmetically challenged ramps make it into the tote in the name of speed (they are sorted out before final packing, and end up as home-use).

Note: If you own a hardwood stand, consider growing leeks. If you already have agreements with landowners to harvest, they will probably be open to letting you take starter clumps, or expanding their own areas.

EXTENDING THE SEASON

As Earth tilts and the northern hemisphere gets more sun, the good 'ramper' follows the fresh leeks north. There are certain tricks to use as it gets toward the end of the season to stretch it out for just a few more days. You've got to maintain quality right up to the end. Sometimes it's a slow spiral down the well of diminishing returns, other times it's over over-night.

To some people, one or two hundred dollars a day may not be a lot of money. Good for them. For Karen and me it is a golden opportunity. When we know that we may only have a few weeks to make those amounts, we keep our schedule clear. We have tuned our lives in to the way the season progresses, from cold days and small leeks, to warmer longer days and yellow leaf tips. The good times in-between at any given location are short.

A list of weather related things that can affect sales; frost, drought, heat, sleet, sheets of rain, snow, winds—any and all of which can occur in a single season. These are usually widespread events so they can create extra work for the harvester all season.

One year, the first leeks were up when a super cold night hit. Depending on the particular location anywhere between 20% and 80% of the potential crop was ruined. You always have to be selective and take only the nicest looking ones but this was affecting all of the biggest ramps. Another year, the whole state had a sleet storm!

On the other hand we were once saved by a snow storm in the middle of the season when it insulated the leaves against a subsequent hard frost. Leeks are amazingly cold hardy though, withstanding temps in the low 20's.

The later in the season it gets, the more important an attention to details becomes. You have to know your options and your limits, and when to call it quits. A few good tricks might make a few hundred dollars. I won't go into all of them here, just the ice. Cold water in the totes (the colder the better) helps preserve freshness. In April, it's often cold enough to go without ice, but if it warms up, it's worth it to buy each tote a bag of ice, or even two.

Note; harvested product loses its cold-hardiness. Do not expose their leaves to anything below freezing. I've even seen frost damage to leaves that were in totes with lids on (Ice in the water on the bulbs is fine).

OILING THE RAMP MACHINE

Teamwork

Working as a team has its advantages, and its pitfalls. One common problem crops up when you have more leeks than you do buyers. The thing to do would be to put the operation on hold while trying to find another outlet for the product.

Another problem can occur when one person is delivering other peoples product, and someone didn't clean good enough. The penalty for delivering dirty leeks has been a cut in pay, or having to stay at the distributor and re-rinse them all.

Yet another downfall can occur when one link in the chain brings quality down in such a way that it isn't immediately apparent. If the delivery person lets the product get warm, if the rinsing crew is careless, or if the harvester misses any of a number of chances to keep quality up, expect to pay. If everyone's were lumped in together, it may look like you are all delivering poor quality product. Chefs will complain about it and demand a refund.

It's not all bad though. Teamwork works under nurturing conditions. Even a loose partnership between two or three gatherers can pay off in unforeseen ways when various people's abilities balance each other.

THE CLEANERS

We changed our way of harvesting and cleaning in mid-season several years ago. The old method began by pulling off the ramp's bulb sheath as soon as they were dug up. Then we put them neatly into a milk crate (or a clothes basket with holes drilled in the bottom).The crate was then dunked in a water bath and jostled back and forth to rinse off the dirt from the roots.

At home, the crates were sprayed through (from side and bottom) with hose and nozzle. Then we stored them in the shade in a water-bath for up to three days while we harvested more.

For the long trip to Lansing, a water-bath was made in the bed of the truck or trailer into which the crates were placed. A lid or covering of some sort was necessary to keep the wind off the leeks. The water flowing through the crates as the vehicle took corners and hills would further rinse the leeks. By the time they were pulled from the bath, they were fairly clean. (If this final bath was to work, you had to do a good job of pre-rinsing everyone's crates or else the dirty ones would contaminate the others).

When we started selling our product to another distributor, the above method had to be modified since it did not get the leeks quite clean enough. The switchover was prompted by a set of promises from the other distributor. Lucky it was easy enough to make the changes with our existing resources.

Now, all of our cleaning takes place at headquarters. This method means you can harvest more in an hour, but cleaning takes longer. We look for someone who will dedicate themselves to wash ramps every day if need be. That means we can maximize our time digging. Washing, is done with a hose and sprayer. We leave the skins on until we get everything laid out on the table.

In a pinch, it can be done at night by electric light, but it is colder and more trouble. We have often had to stop as dark starts to settle in, not because we couldn't see, but because ice was forming on the leaves from the rinse-water.

Rinsing can also be a good team operation, so we like to have a second person on call for those *days Mama warned us about*. Two cleaners can stay ahead of four people harvesting. We also end up washing our own when circumstances keep us out of the woods for a day.

We pay a full time washer $10.00 just for showing up to work the day, plus .50 cents per pound. We hire their services out to other diggers for .60 cents per pound (the extra dime going to us to help defray our system costs).

Beware of the tendency to harvest more than you will be able to wash on time. Buyers often want to move an agreed upon delivery time, according to whatever factors they may be dealing with in their world. Times may move forward by a day or more, causing a cleaning 'crunch'.

Rejects. Ahem . . . home-use. We pluck out less-than-perfect specimens for a variety of reasons; broken stems, sliced bulbs etc. We divide the many pounds of home-use amongst the crew.

THE BIG WASH

We have constructed a long stationary table for washing hundreds of pounds of leeks. It is within easy reach of a hose from our house well. We mount several lights on high poles for working at night. There is plenty of shade nearby for the packaged product. The table itself is narrow, about 14inches wide. It slopes away from the hose handler so that water flows off readily. A two-inch wide gap runs the length of it, also to help with drainage. It's important to build it at the right height for ease of working.

The cleaning crew 2012; Josh & Larry—striving to maximize efficiency, speed and cleanliness. We fit up to 25 lbs. on the table at one time. Skins are pulled from the lower side.

We regularly dig with other people in some sort of partnership. If they don't have a place to rinse their own product we rent the use of this setup for them to wash their own ramps. We charge ten cents a pound for the use of it. The spot is in use almost every day when leek season rolls around. The system is also useful it at other times of the year for cleaning various other crops we get in quantity.

It took many purchases before we came up with the ideal combination of splitter and sprayer. The brass nozzle delivers a powerful jet of water for cleaning bulbs.

Set up your own area with the above considerations in mind, or tailor it to fit your own situation. Just remember, there will be a lot of water used in a day and it has to go somewhere. In our case, it soaks into the sod. It helps that the ground slopes away from the work area. Even so, most of us wear rubber boots and rain pants.

Our system can be readied quite quickly at the beginning of each workday. A nearby picnic table provides a convenient place to set several totes—one with leeks that need cleaning, one for clean leeks to go into and a third full of water for a final dunk.

Note that the leeks are held in place by weighting their leaves with short narrow boards while we work.

How To Ready Product for Market   Note: This works if you do not have a cooler. If you DO have a cooler, you can eliminate certain steps.

1. Drain a tote of leeks to be cleaned by slowly tilting it up on its side. Let all of the dirty water drain as you keep the leeks from falling out. Keep drained totes on end for ease of removing leeks.

2. Reject damaged leeks as you go: spotty, yellowing, bruised, or holey leaves and/or sliced or crushed bulbs. Bulbs without roots are not rejects if the bulbs are intact. Our goal for good product upon delivery is between 96% and 100%. Watch for rejects at all stages of washing/packing. Note: rejected leeks are often good enough for home-use*.

3. When laying leeks on table, keep bulbs back from lower edge by about 2 inches. Layer two or three leeks deep. Keep bulbs even throughout washing process (especially when re-packing). Be aware that those few tall leaves that hang over the upper edge are subject to damage if you aren't careful.

4. Gently place boards on leaves to hold them down. Beware breezes. Leaves are rubbery, so as long as there is weight on them they should stay put.

5. Pull skins off bulbs. Break off roots/rhizome ONLY if big and ugly. This part of the operation is done from the downhill side only.

6. Always, spray from the uphill side. Spray bulbs from all angles except toward leaves. Avoid blowback of debris up into leaves. Do not hit leaves with full-pressure spray—they damage easy. It is easiest to make three full passes, repositioning the hose direction at the beginning of each pass rather than trying to hit each leek in turn from three directions. As you spray your way from one end of the table to the other, work your fingers through the bulbs to loosen any tenacious dirt.

7. Leaves may also need to be sprayed LIGHTLY after removing boards. (It depends on how dirty they are.) If not, dunk them in clean water by the handfuls as you transfer them to containers. Totes rest on-end while laying leeks in to repack. Thus, when full totes are sat upright, the leeks are standing upright too.

8. "If it ain't tight, it ain't right." Pack totes tightly, bottom to top, but not so tight, that you can't get the ice in without causing damage. Loosely packed leeks get bent. Plan for the size of the day's last container, or use a spacer to keep tight if lacking produce to fill. When full, set tote up and add four or five inches of water.

Packed totes, iced, wrapped and under shade.

9. Use ice on days when above 40°F or if delivery is days away. Keep ice off leaves (it damages them). Store with lids on. Full totes should be kept in shade at all times.

10. Keep rinsed chilled leeks covered with two layers of thick blankets if over 40°F. Also keep covered if below freezing (harvested leeks are especially susceptible to frost). Stack totes tightly. Blankets/tarps should go to the ground and be weighted against the wind.

11. Rinse and gather empty totes and lids as you go.

12. At day's end, clean area and turn off hydrant. Disconnect, drain and hang hose. Turn off lights etc.

* Set up a system for keeping less-than-perfect product that made it into the harvest. We set a tote full of water next to the wash station, into which go the home-use leeks until they can be taken care of.

TRANSPORTATION & DELIVERY

The miles add up like this; hauling ice, getting to the woods in the morning, getting home at night with leeks on board, delivering product every three days, and meeting Joe at the tavern now and then.

A round trip to the woods can range from a couple miles if we are working the 'back 40' to several hundred miles for our farthest fields. A delivery run to the distributor (and back) takes six hours or more. You can only harvest for about 2 or 3 days before you have to wash them and get them to the distributor, or run the risk of spoilage. Once you get them into a cooler, they are good for a week or so.

It took a few tries to work out the right formula for a way to pay a delivery person based on however many pounds they are taking, for whoever may have dug them. A flat rate per trip of $100.00 is easily divided by the percentage each person has of the load total, plus thirty cents per pound for however much a person actually has on board.

Let us say, for example, that we have a 400lb load with three people's product (we won't really know the weights until the driver gets back with the tally). Digger One had 100lbs, Two had 250lbs and Three had 50. One had 25% (or $25 worth) of the load total and $30 worth in weight, and so pays $55 to the driver. Two had 62.5% of the load total and $75 in weight, and so pays the driver $137.50. Three had 1/8th, or 12.5%, and 50lbs. at .30 cents per, and so pays $27.50. The driver's total would then be $220.00.

Earthy Delights and Elegance Distributors are the main competitors for ramp distribution here in the Great Lakes region. It's ironic that their company initials are both E. D., and one of the owners is even named Ed. They both sell many of the same products other than the ramps. We have sold ramps to both of them, and to several other nearer smaller buyers. Each has their own considerations. For instance, the cleaning method may be different for one buyer than for another, depending on the level of cleanliness requested. Either way is fine, but it is the buyer's choice, some will even buy them un-rinsed.

Ready to return from a weekend up north.

We try to put as many hours in the woods as we can, often working until dark. We bring our totes full of dirty ramps home at the end of the day. When it's just the two of us harvesting, everything we need for the day fits in the jeep. We fold the back seats down and by the end of the day we can just about fit the whole day's work back inside.

If we don't have a clean water source at the particular woods where we are working we will transport a barrel full with us. Once a tote is packed full, it must have water poured in. A trip out of the woods with a full day's work on board might make a person think about installing overload springs. So we did.

I mentioned earlier how we used to harvest and ship in crates or baskets. Many wholesale harvesters these days use totes. We also use boxes, buckets and gathering sacks. There are a number of advantages to the plastic tote:

First; they are taller, so there's not as much chance of damaging the long leaves during transport.

Second; they act as self-contained water baths, portable enough to keep in the shade, stackable with their lids on and you can put ice in them to keep them cool.

Third; when it comes time to haul them from the field or to the distributor, there is almost no mess, so you can load them right into your vehicle and go (no need to make a water bath in the bed of the truck or trailer).

The only notable disadvantage with the plastic totes is the price. Do get the good ones the first time around *or you'll be sorry*. Some buyers supply totes to their regular harvesters.

If you can find a local ice business, negotiate for ice in bulk. If you make the trip to pick it up, you might get half off the price.

Once the product is out of our hands, it is shipped hither and yon by various means, even by air.

THE SAFE SIDE

Since there is the chance of microbial food contamination for fresh consumed foods, here's how to lessen the risk:

When we harvest ramps for sale, we don't know who will be eating them. We don't know who will be preparing them. We don't know how they will be prepared, or when. If we knew for sure that they were going to be cooked, we wouldn't have to worry as much, but sometimes ramps are served raw.

Contamination by pathogens results from an external source at some point from production to preparation. For ramps as with all fruits and vegetables consumed without a cooking step, it is best to be aware of the potential problems and to minimize the chance of contamination at every step from harvest to sale.

Remember, prevention is favored over treatments to eliminate microbial contamination that may have already occurred, because once contaminated, removing or killing pathogens on produce is very difficult. There are many opportunities for bacteria, viruses, and parasites to contaminate produce. Soil, manure, water, animals, equipment, and workers may all spread harmful organisms.

Does it go without saying that domestic animals should be excluded from harvesting areas during growing and harvest season? It is a simple principle for minimizing animal fecal contamination. It is not possible to eliminate all animal influences from ramp production fields however. Deer will often be seen leaving the area when we arrive. All we can do is steer wide of their droppings when we find them. Several areas where we work are adjacent to farm fields that are dressed annually with fresh manure from the farmer's cows. The ramps along the edges look great, but we do not take them when the farmer has been there before us.

Pathogens such as E. coli, salmonella, and campylobacter can be present in manure slurry and soil for three months or more, depending on temperature and soil conditions. Listeria can survive on vegetables growing in the

119

soil, even though it may not survive in the soil itself. Avoid areas near or downstream from animal holding operations where runoff occurs into the woods.

If getting water at the harvest site for keeping roots wet for the day, avoid ponds and swamp-water. Plan ahead—when working far from home, we have had to buy water from the locals. Now, we often haul a clean barrel of our own water to the woods. A quick flowing creek may be ok if you're lucky enough to be working near one, but I always take a walk upstream to check the source to be sure (any excuse for a walk in the woods is good enough for me). Water may look clear, even with a deer carcass upstream in the oxbow. It may smell fine, even full of giardia from the beaver pond up around the bend.

Besides microbial contamination, there is the possibility of chemical drift from farm fields and orchards. Wild food foragers should realize that this problem could affect many of their favorites. Along power lines and railways, at parks and in residential yards, who knows what strange chemicals people may have sprayed to keep the undergrowth down.

Watch out for dumps too. We were working a wood once on an old farmer's back forty where multiple barrels marked "hazardous" lay strewn along the tree line. We proceeded deeper into the woods.

On the subject of contamination, there is no substitute for personal hygiene and good health amongst all workers who come into contact with any food product. Establish a program that includes proper hand washing and a clear policy that workers who report or are observed to have symptoms of illness are to be reassigned to activities that do not involve food or food surface contact.

Further, all equipment that touches fresh produce must be treated as food contact surfaces. Establish cleaning and sanitizing programs for all such surfaces. Ensure that harvest crews are aware of microbial risk reduction and principles, and adhere to established food safety practices. Clean all food contact surfaces and remove as much dirt as practicable from harvest containers prior to use.

And remember that the quality of postharvest water that contacts fresh produce during cleaning and cooling is widely recognized as the central control point for fresh produce. Ensure that water is of adequate quality throughout all packing operations from start to finish, ice too.

Keep produce cool at all times after harvest, cool it quickly and store at appropriate temperatures to maintain quality. Make sure that all water used for ice, cooling, washing and hauling operations is drinkable (potable).

Finally, limit cross-contamination during transportation and distribution. Inspect delivery vehicles for cleanliness and odors prior to loading.

IT'S ALWAYS SOMETHING

Having said all of the above about microbes, contamination, and cleanliness, I would again point out the Allium family's natural resistances. They tend to subdue most pathogens on contact.

Still, in 2003, more than 650 people were sickened and four died from hepatitis A, contracted from Mexican green onions served in a Chi-Chi's near Pittsburgh, Pennsylvania. That's right, onions. The FDA attributed the outbreak to poor sanitation. The total compensation paid by the chain was $50 million.

Tens of thousands of illnesses, costing hundreds of millions in health-related costs occur annually from just one such germ, E. coli, the leading cause of food-borne infections. Consumers have repeatedly demonstrated that they will hold all segments of the food supply chain accountable for food-borne illnesses.

The most harmful of potential contaminants that can cause food-borne illnesses are disease-causing microbes of human or animal origin, 'germs'. There are three common causes of action in food-borne illness lawsuits:

1. Product Liability—in which the injured plaintiff must prove that the product was defective and unreasonably dangerous when it left the food suppliers control and that the defect was the 'proximate cause' of the injury.
2. Breach of Warranty—in which the plaintiff may claim that the product does not conform to an express or implied warranty and the nonconformance caused the injury.
3. Negligence—in which food suppliers may be held liable because of negligence on their part that contaminated the food and caused purchasers of the food to become ill.

KEEPING IT GREEN— DREAMS & FESTIVALS

"Yes your Honor, I was arrested for taking a leek in the woods." Niles

Wild foods expert and author of Wild Plants I Have Known...and Eaten, Russ Cohen says, "entire colonies of ramps are being dug up in the Berkshires, leaving a barren patch of ground, a practice that is clearly not sustainable and leaving no possibility for regeneration."

Since the Native Americans first introduced European settlers to the native flora, the ongoing utilization and sometimes exploitation of North America's plant-life is historical fact. Two hundred native plant species are at risk of extinction in the United States due to gathering for consumption, half of them are herbaceous forest perennials. Allium tricoccum may soon be one of them. Annual intensive harvesting of ramps is seriously damaging wild populations.

Studies demonstrate that sustainable harvests take only a small amount (less than 5% annually) from a given population. This is not an easy number to judge if harvesting on public lands where multiple harvesters may come and go.

The ramps consumed at festivals and at gourmet restaurants, are all gathered from the wild, often from our public forests. Increased harvests in the Smoky Mountain

National Park, in North Carolina and Tennessee prompted a ban there in 2002. More recently, the Nantahala National Forest has had restrictions placed on ramp harvests. It's not surprising either since studies show that ramp populations need many years to recover from a single heavy harvest. I expect to see more restrictions throughout their range in the near future.

The cultivation of ramps can be relatively rapid and easy compared to other long-lived woodland plants but such efforts remain in the fledgling stages. The vast majority of ramps are therefore taken directly from an ever-decreasing wild reserve.

There is no reason to believe that the demand for ramps will decrease any time soon either, since there has been a steady increase in the demand for large, consistent supplies. Thus, in an effort to conserve native populations and meet rising demand, a number of possible solutions are recommended. Sustainable harvesting, reducing waste, suppression of invasive species and cultivation of ramps are all voluntary measures that any of us can have a part in. Ultimately, it may take regulation.

POPULATION RECOVERY STUDIES

Botanists are concerned about the future of ramps and cite the plants shared traits with other now at-risk species. As with other perennial forest herbs, conservation requires information on the effects of harvesting on populations and recovery rates.

A study was conducted at The Great Smoky Mountains National Park in the southern Appalachian Mountains bordering North Carolina and Tennessee. Three sites, which were located in the central portion of the park and had not been regularly visited by harvesters, were selected. Plots were established at each site. Differing harvest levels were applied to each and monitored over a four-year period (1989-1993).

Before harvest, leaf widths were measured, (leaf widths are good indicators of plant age and bulb size). Measurements were used to estimate growth rates and population recovery times for each site.

Harvesting reduced average leaf widths, with the magnitude of the effect related to the degree of the initial population reduction, suggesting that populations did not recover within the 4-year study period. Theoretical recovery times were thus estimated for differing harvest intensities. The study concluded that harvesting is not sustainable except at very modest levels. Sustainable harvest levels were assumed to be 10% or less, once every 10 years.

Another research project by the British Ecological Society, also suggests that even a small harvest can have a big impact. The studies in Quebec led to a commercial harvesting ban for the entire province, (small amounts are allowed for personal use). Three US states have also listed ramps as plants of special concern. Will these few bans be all, or has a trend toward widespread regulation of ramps begun? Poached ramps anyone?

Long time harvesting is having an effect upon ramp populations. It doesn't take scientific studies for experienced harvesters to know when patches have been over-harvested. I have seen the effects of my own heavy harvests. I learned to expand my territory, and to move through a given area in less time.

INVASION PHENOMENON

The time is far-gone when our world of resources could be thought of as unending. The time is gone when we had individual environmental problems on which to focus. For some time now, we have been realizing that since all life is inter-existent, then so too are all the problems we face that we alone have created.

Environmental problems have a way of affecting people in ways they would not have guessed. My family started a cross-country ski resort in 1976. We ran an eco-friendly business, but global warming ran us out of it. Now I hear that forested areas in Michigan could decline as much as 50-70% because of climate change. These forests are my retreat, my livelihood and my home. Just as important, maybe more, they are home to elk, bear and wolf—to plants and fungi. And to many other *Michiganders* they provide benefits from tourism, recreation, timber products and more.

On top of global warming, the wildcrafter has an ongoing fight with invasive species. Many non-natives do not cause problems. However, some reproduce and spread into wild habitats, becoming dominant. Native species and entire communities of plants and animals are often displaced.

The rate at which invasive species may invade a forest is based on a number of factors, particularly the size and remoteness of the forest, and the proximity and size of the populations of non-native plants. Disturbance to the woodland habitat by ramp harvesters can increase the ability of invasive plants to spread. Ramps are subject to natural displacement in the forest when conditions change. Trees fall, light brings briars, ramps retreat. It's no surprise that they are also susceptible to invasion by non-native species such as exotic grasses and garlic mustard.

Ethnobotonist Lawrence Davis-Hollander warns that displacement has been observed where ramps have been disturbed. "Digging creates a surface of open soil suitable for exotic seed germination, and produces gaps in relatively stable and invasive resistant clumps. Botanists have noticed that when a colony of plants is left undisturbed it may flourish and remain intact for a very long time, a phenomena known as stability. Once the invasive species take root in a clump of ramps they reduce the possibilities of the native plants reestablishing themselves. Relatively little is known scientifically about what happens over time to a clump of ramps or other woodland wildflowers, once disturbed . . ."

Invasives compromise native habitats through competition, interfering with mycorrhizal (plant root-fungi) relationships and by releasing allelopathic elements into the soil. In addition, with few exceptions, only those insects that have a long shared evolutionary past with a particular plant have developed the physiological adaptations needed to digest the chemicals in their host's foliage.

The most effective way to protect your local forests from invading species is by prevention. When buying garden plants, avoid those that are invasive. Remember that wind and water can carry them far from your home, into wild habitats. If you live near a natural area be especially watchful for invasive species! Also, if you are in any kind of land management or ownership position, do whatever you can to prevent fragmentation. Small parcels are more susceptible to invasion.

Other factors, which may have predictably bad effects on ramp populations, are pollution, a warming climate, overgrazing and lumbering—all of which are good news for invasives. A cascade of chaos is occurring throughout the forest, which has never had the chance to recover from humankind's previous assaults. Sort of takes the kind out of mankind . . .

In his article, Gardening for Life, Douglas Tallamy, University of Delaware professor and chair of the Entomology & Wildlife Ecology Department encourages landowners to join the fight to reestablish a native natural order. The ecosystems that support us—that determine the carrying capacity of the earth and our local spaces—are run by biodiversity.

Professor Tallamy explains why we need biodiversity. Not just an abundance of different species either—the right species in the right relationship is the goal. "With human induced climate change threatening the planet, it is biodiversity that will suck that carbon out of the air and sequester it in living plants if given half a chance. Humans cannot live as the only species on this planet because it is *other species* that create the ecosystem services essential to us. Every time we force a species to extinction, we are encouraging our own demise. Despite the disdain with which we have treated it in the past, biodiversity is not optional."

RAMPS AT RISK?

Our species has driven to extinction, medicinal plants worth tens of billions of dollars annually in the United States alone. As one who makes a living with endangered wild plants, Richo Cech, author of Growing at-Risk Medicinal Herbs offers a personal observation. "Herbalists are challenged to serve the burgeoning human population while at the same time, the wild plant populations, the main source of our traditional materia medica, diminish at an alarming rate . . . beyond concern over the economic losses caused by plant extinctions, there is clearly a personal, cultural, scientific, medical and aesthetic value in maintaining the health of our wild places and in fostering our wild plants."

He continues, "the dwindling supply of many wild herbs has resulted in their regulation by the convention for international trade in endangered species of wild fauna and flora. A CITES listing tends to slow exportation of the herb, although only in the raw form . . . Monitoring wild populations, educating the public about the source of the herbs used to make their medicines and researching appropriate cultivation methodologies would more successfully protect these wild resources."

He's not talking specifically about ramps, but the following paragraph sums up the relationship. "Populations of wild annual or biannual plants that reproduce readily from seed are generally sustainable even in the face of wholesale harvest. There is usually an intact seed bank in the soil that produces ample re-growth for next year, and seeds may even lie dormant in the soil for decades until the right germination conditions are encountered. However, the harvest of a long-lived perennial plant has much greater impact, because it can take many years for the plant to be replaced in nature. Older seed bearing individuals are the depositories for the genetic and regenerative potential of the population." And as we know, ramps are in the second category.

Mr. Cech's book focuses on twenty of the top endangered medicinals. What do ramps have in common with the plants that comprise the United Plant Savers at-risk list? They come from distinct habitats, their environments are under siege by development, grazing and/or logging, and they are long-lived, perennial plants that may not reproduce quickly or reliably when older seed bearing specimens are harvested.

Conservationists have long labored to show the economic value in caring for and preserving natural and cultural heritage. As Ernest Dickerman, granddad of the eastern wilderness said, "You have to keep right on pointing out how important it is to preserve the wild country. People are always a lot more interested in the short-term economic benefits rather than the long-term quality-of-life issues."

People (us) must admit when they (we) are wrong. In fact we must be readily seeking out our wrongs and happily state them as we correct them. Not only should we do this as individuals but as couples and groups and coalitions and nations, and as a race.

We can't be afraid of making mistakes (everyone does anyway). We should be afraid of not having the courage to admit them. Better to do so, than to be forcibly corrected by outside forces. I used to take a few too many ramps from a given area. I still sell them, but now I plant them too.

A voluntary effort could save ramps and many other endangered species, but whether voluntary or not they all deserve protection and respect. But for it to actually work, heroic efforts must be made. There will soon be no diversity to maintain unless we reverse course. World leaders, lawgivers, regulators, business execs and ordinary people by the billions must share responsibility for the well-being of the planet.

I've seen the trillium making a slow comeback, so I do have hope.

OLD RULES NEW RULES

Private landowners have the biggest responsibility to preserve natural ecosystems, and to reestablish them where possible, because they own most of the land, and that is what it's going to take. Second-growth forests have been thoroughly invaded by alien plants. Many of these invaders came from our own yards. If we hope to avoid a global mass extinction from which we also are not likely to recover, we need to replace unnecessary lawns and golf courses with densely planted woodlots that can serve as habitat for our local biodiversity.

One would hope that this would all take place voluntarily. Americans have always valued private liberty. On public lands though, we all have a say.

It is not technically legal to harvest any whole plant in a national park. Ramp harvesters however have often been a special exception, similar to mushroomers. There are many more ramps than mushrooms, and many more mushroomers than ramp harvesters.

In North Carolina's national forests, it is legal to pick up to five pounds of ramps per individual per year with a free permit. In North Carolina alone, usage estimates for all purposes combined are more than 6,000 pounds annually. Commercial permits can be had for up to 500 pounds at fifty cents per pound. This program could work for most states where ramps grow.

I tend to believe that there are presently ample supplies of ramps overall, but that many more areas are becoming overharvested or damaged otherwise. Some areas are doomed not to recover. The ramp's range will shrink and become fragmented. A slow trend of depletion will leave remaining stands ever more vulnerable to all of the dangers previously mentioned. Eventually even the vast patches on public lands will be stretched thin. By then an industry sector will have disappeared. By then we could have gone in a different direction, if we start now.

More states will control commercial ramp harvests, or begin to enforce existing laws. Do I welcome the inevitable? What choice do I have? It's part of the bigger fight we all face—the fight between our wishes to eat our cake and have it too.

WHO REALLY CARES?

I think that it means we have to care about what it is that's at stake. To do that we have to think beyond our ephemeral short-term benefits. For many people that can be an overwhelming proposition because they feel that they are in the same position as the environment we are talking about saving; undervalued, displaced, raped and ignored. And certainly that is true for some.

But just what is at stake? Wild leeks are just one small part of the picture. Anyone with an ear with which to listen has surely heard of our certain doom. As sure as there's a formula for DDT, there is a recipe for environmental destruction, and few people put it as well as Anne and Paul Ehrlich in their 1970s Mother Earth News 'Ecoscience' series: "All over the globe, at an ever-increasing pace, populations of all sorts of organisms are being paved over, plowed under, grazed away, flooded out, strip-mined, poisoned, invaded, and—above all destroyed as forests are cleared . . . The services provided by ecosystems, as you may recall, include such essentials as the amelioration of the climate, the disposal of wastes and recycling of nutrients, the generation and maintenance of soils, and the control of the vast majority of crop pests and transmitters of human diseases. Humanity has no satisfactory way of replacing these free services should they be lost . . . and civilization cannot persist without them."

In his series Ramps: When is Local not Kosher, Lawrence Davis-Hollander reports, "one purveyor, Earthy Delights, begins getting group shipments from small harvesters in the southeast, of about 600-700 pounds trucked from each region, with main season shipments of 1,000 lbs every ten to fourteen days. They sell direct to the consumer at around $9.50 – $12.00 per pound. The majority of their stock goes to chefs. No one has established how many ramps are presently dug every year, and assembling precise statistics would be difficult. Another harvester in New York State produces 18,000-20,000 pounds or approximately 1-1.5 million plants for the New York City market. They claim to be mapping their harvest activity, and removing plants on a five year rotational basis in order to insure sustainability. While I do not have complete information it is hard to believe that such quantities are not reducing ramp populations. Botanists, harvesters and purveyors agree that demand has skyrocketed during the last few years."

A loss of habitat is often resultant from a loss of species. Whenever species go extinct, a serious consequence is registered in the loss of the ecosystem services once provided by those creatures. Moreover, evolutionary biologists have shown that the space required to sustain biodiversity is pretty much the same as the area required to create it in the first place.

So, a loss of species is often resultant from a loss of habitat.

We humans are not the center of the universe—our needs rank pretty low on the planet's agenda. We seem more like a parasite than the sentient race we profess to be.

Sorry.

Still, our needs are important to us.

Undeniably, though, many of the things we are now forced to do without were once considered needed, not just wanted. Indeed, we have shown that we will do things as a race (or mob) that a single reasoning person would never do. By our slow-but-sure erasure of one over-needed species after another, we have cost ourselves a place in paradise—is there even room in the same sentence to mention the enormous economic benefits we have cost ourselves?

Only about 1% of the total number of higher plant species has ever been found useful by people for food, of which a mere 150 or so have been commercially grown, and every one of which is a precious resource. We should be adding new plants to that list, not striking them off.

Are ramps being harvested sustainably? Probably yes for those few to be used on a personal basis. Maybe not for those sold at farmers' markets—maybe not for the thousands of pounds that supply the many festivals, and most likely not for the many tons sold to high-end restaurants. Thing is . . . none of the above uses are inherently bad. They should all be encouraged.

Question is, "can they be harvested sustainably?"

Of course they can! Nature does it already, and she is our great teacher. It's just a matter of where, of how and how much.

Falling trees thin ramps mercilessly.

SOME RECOMMENDATIONS

Those that express concern at the manner and rate of commercial ramp harvesting also note that there is a long history in the southeast of harvesting for personal use, roadside sales and festivals. Traditional harvest methods leave patches relatively intact. Collection done exclusively by knowledgeable wild food foragers has possibly the greatest chance for conservation.

New commercial collectors are entering the market with no experience in collecting plants. They see ramps as a quick buck. Unless they are provided with proper knowledge, they may never develop an understanding of the long-term consequences of their actions.

North Carolina State University horticulturist Dr. Jeanine Davis suggests a traditional Cherokee method of harvesting leaves and the attached petiole (*stem*). This may be a viable alternative to bulb harvesting. The clumps would remain intact. Further, the leaves require virtually no cleaning; the petiole provides a crunchy texture and tastes excellent. However, she cautions, "over-harvest of leaves could over a long time period be as deleterious as the whole plant harvest, depriving ramps of the ability to grow and maintain vigor."

Lawrence Davis-Hollander singles out the culinary community, and asks them to "cease the promotion and sale of wild leeks." He urges harvesters gathering for family and friends to focus on leaf harvest."If you absolutely must have some bulbs then consider a handful or two, not pounds." He also entreats the ramp festival culture to lead efforts to "monitor, preserve and increase current ramp populations without increasing the current rate of harvest. If ramp festivals utilized leaves that could reduce their harvests by as much as 30%."

Farming ramps has promise for saving them, and other less obvious benefits. Harvesting ramps from managed plantings would profit many people; Farmers with an idle woodlot, foresters who could market ramps like they do timber and harvesters, who often end up traveling to remote locations. Native populations would regenerate. Ramps would gain respect and recognition with consumers. Prices would stabilize.

Ramps can be cultivated in their native habitats. Seed can take 6 to18 months to germinate. It takes about 7 or 8 years to produce a mature plant. But will it be profitable? We know how to grow and harvest other crops sustainably.

Usually there's some monetary incentive. I think that in the long run ramps will prove to be profitable enough that more people will grow them.

Licensing would keep inexperienced harvesters off public lands. A license to dig ramps could be issued to those who are willing to follow certain guidelines. I can envision a handful of ways it could work. Other programs exist in other states, which could be copied in all states. However it is done, *the sooner the better*.

And it has to be everywhere ramps grow, or it would be worse than no regulations at all. Just not for the perception of fairness, but for the fact that harvesters already follow the wave of green across state lines as it moves north. Leeks in the states or provinces surrounding one where there are restrictions would suffer because of pressures from those harvesters who are displaced from their traditional grounds. Experience in Quebec has shown that the law does not always stop poachers. They find a ready market where there are no regulations across the border in Ontario.

"How we eat determines to a considerable extent how the world is used." Wendell Berry.

GROW YOUR OWN

"Forest gardens are immensely productive and offer many benefits. These systems incorporate an upper story of trees for timber, fruits, and nuts, a middle story of bushes producing fruits and spices, and an understory of maize, beans, and root crops. A community that relies on forest gardens as opposed to tillage systems uses far less energy, reduces soil erosion significantly, and supports more stable and diverse ecosystems." From the book, Balance Point by Joseph C. Jenkins.

The North Carolina Extension Service published one of several available 'growing guides'. Obviously there's some interest in farming A. tricoccum, and as was shown in the previous chapter there is a pressing need. The guide's authors proclaim, "in an effort to conserve native populations and meet the rising demand, we are developing cultivation practices for ramps. Harvesting ramps from easily accessible, concentrated plantings would not only benefit festival participants, chefs, and consumers, but also create a new marketable product for the commercial grower.

There are so many good reasons to plant ramps . . . Not as many good ways to go about it. I will be presenting only the method for propagation by bulb transplanting, as this is the only method I have any experience with. Also, it is to my mind the most effective method. It means an immediate seed source and provides harvestable ramps in 2 to 3 years.

While research is in progress to develop the most efficient, practical, and sustainable production practices for ramps, information on growing them is still limited. Studies and experience indicate that ramps *can* be successfully cultivated for commercial purposes. Glen Facemire's Ramp Farm is one example. A long-term commitment on the grower's part is advised, and a mature forest setting is critical to ensure healthy populations. Amending the soil may improve production.

CHOOSING A SITE

A thickly wooded area provides an ideal location for planting ramps. Look for areas that are already home to plants that they associate with, such as nettle, toothwort, bellwort, bloodroot, trout lily and others. Avoid areas thick with saplings, briars or other encroaching under growth.

Ramps grow best in a hardwood forest of sugar maple, beech, birch, and/or poplar (heavy on the maple). Other trees under which ramps will grow include buckeye, basswood, cherry, hickory and the occasional oak.

Even a steep hillside will work, if the trees are of the right age and mix.

Keep in mind that having adequate light, moisture and nutrients for the few weeks in the spring when ramps leaf out is essential. Studies show that raising calcium levels initially is beneficial for establishment. Ramps prefer soils with high calcium: magnesium ratios and an average soil pH of 5.5.

Choose a well-drained site with moist, rich soil. Moisture content is an important determiner for seed germination, seedling emergence rate, survival and yearly growth rate. Even if you are planting bulbs, eventually the plants will cast their own seed. Thus, adequate soil moisture is important all year, not just in the growing season. The soil should be naturally high in organic matter such as leaves and other decaying plant material from the forest.

One disadvantage in transplanting the bulbs is their cost. Seeds are cheaper. If you gather your own seeds, they are free and easy it you time it right.

You can also gather your own bulbs, which I encourage. You will have the best survival rate with bulbs that you have dug with the sole purpose of transplanting them.

If you do dig your own, you have to choose a site from which to get them. If you have options, take them from a spot where they are being crowded out, or from where the soil type is not quite right (too much clay etc.).

TIMING

Seeds have a dormant, under-developed embryo, which requires a warm, moist period and then a subsequent cold period to break their dormant stage. The seed will often wait until the second spring to germinate.

However, replanting mats of bulbs allows for same year seed production. Bulbs for transplanting can be dug between September and April. Late February to early April is the best time, depending on your latitude, for transplanting young plants. Once the ground has thawed, dig gently, taking care not to damage the bulbs, roots or rhizome.

Digging methods for transplanting are not exactly the same as those described in the chapter on harvesting for eating. Care should be taken to leave the bulbs in bunches of four to eight plants each. While harvesting, keep them cool and moist. When harvest is complete, do not wash, and do not trim off the rootlets. Do not store in airtight containers.

Clump ready for transplanting

SITE PREP AND PLANTING

Rake back the leaves on the forest floor, removing any unwanted weeds, tree sprouts, rocks or roots. Loosen the soil to prepare a small circular bed. Dig out the center to approximately 3 inches deep, and form a bowl. Lay the bulbs in the depression pressing the clump gently into the soil. Use extra dirt to bury the clump to its original depth, keeping just the tips of the bulb above the surface. Planting depth is important for survival. If transplanting leafed-out plants put them at the same depth, at which they had been growing. Clumps of 4 to 8 bulbs can be grouped as close as four clumps per square yard.

Cover with several inches of leaves to retain moisture in the soil and to protect the bulbs from wildlife. We mulch our garden in a similar manner. People look at me incredulously when I tell them how we garden. They start looking for ways that it wouldn't work for them. But the secret is in the mulch, and we get some satisfaction in knowing that Mother Nature mulches too.

A grouping of clumps ready for mulch. Notice the snow?

We got the idea from a couple of books by Ruth Stout, The No Work Garden Book, and How to have a Green Thumb without a Aching Back. These books are worth their weight in gold for anyone who gardens. When I think of all the hours I used to work, fighting nature, expecting to win, I can only say, "that's what I was taught to do." Several years ago, I learned a different trick by a pair of books from a little old lady. Since following Mrs. Stout's gardening advice I've retired my roto-tiller and my hoe. We also use less water and less manure.

Spring spears coming up through the 'duff'.

Hardwood leaves provide the best mulch for ramps. Do not use pine bark or needles, or commercial mulches. The multiple effects of mulching are incredible: Decaying organic matter provides essential elements, moisture is retained, and the mulch helps protect the plants from sub-zero temperatures. In addition, mulching helps to suppress weeds and protects new transplants from wildlife.

After mulching, water your transplants unless it is going to rain within 12hrs, or if the soil is not already wet.

PROBLEMS, PESTS AND DISEASE

Little information is available on such things. Personally I have seen very limited amounts of any problems when ramps are simply left alone. Minor deer and caterpillar damage, and the occasional (septoria) leaf spots occur in wild and cultivated ramps. It may be unsightly but shouldn't adversely affect plant yields.

New plantings do not compete well with weeds, thus weeds should be controlled until the plants are well rooted. If planting in ground that may not be as moist as is optimal, be prepared to water your transplants.

ACKNOWLEDGMENTS

This book could not exist if not for Karen. So blame her if you don't like it. She gave me space, advice and encouragement. She took many of the pictures. She does the work of two people around here, and finds time to help me do a bunch of typing too. I couldn't hope for a better friend and partner.

Joe's friend Niles has the distinction of having taken more leeks in the woods in one day than anyone we know—104 lbs after clean up! Thanks to Niles for the inspiration for the book's sub-title.

Thanks also, to the countless contributors of advice on what this book should say, or not say. Those friends and fellow wildcrafters, and the helpers we have hired over the years have all been heard.

Half of this book comes from outside my own experience. I tried to use direct quotes where they worked, but I would also like to expressly recognize, thank and recommend the following sources:

Skills for Taming The Wild, Bradford Angier

Population Recovery of Wild Leek Allium Tricoccum Following Differential Harvesting In The Southern Appalachians of North Carolina and Tennessee, Rock J.H., Beckage B. & Gross L.J. (2004) Published by the North Carolina Cooperative Extension

Cultivation Of Ramps, Jackie Greenfield, Agricultural Research Technician and Jeanine M. Davis, Extension Horticultural Specialist Department of Horticultural Science in collaboration with the N.C. Department of Agriculture and Consumer Services Plant Protection Division

Growing at-Risk Medicinal Herbs, Richo Cech

Ramps: When is Local not Kosher, Lawrence Davis-Hollander

How Good *Are* Wild Foods?, Robert Shosteck

Balance Point, Joseph C. Jenkins

Gardening For Life, Douglas Tallamy

Edible and Medicinal Plants of the Great Lakes, Thomas A. Naegele

Indian Herbology of North America, Alma R. Hutchens